The Twilight Seas

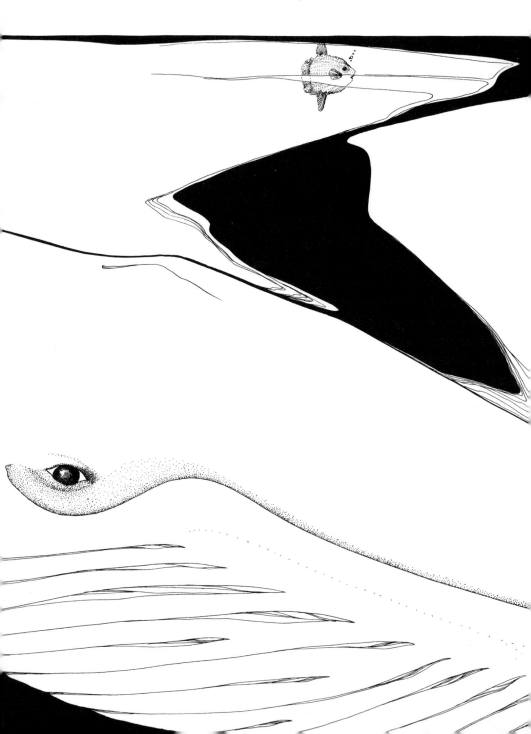

Illustrations by Peter Parnall

SALLY CARRIGHAR

The Twilight Seas

WEYBRIGHT and TALLEY

NEW YORK

Weybright and Talley
750 Third Avenue
New York, New York 10017

Library of Congress Catalog Card Number: 74-83697
ISBN: 0-679-40081-8
MANUFACTURED IN THE UNITED STATES OF AMERICA
Designed by Bob Antler

To the late Robert Murphy,
whose books
The Stream, The Peregrine Falcon
and others
give to readers the rich and magical
sense-experience of wildness.

Contents

The Twilight Seas

I

A World to Delight

At last the Blue Whale was going to be born. After nearly eleven months in the warm nest of his mother's body he had reached the right time to come forth—but the day itself turned out to be most unfortunate.

He had been ready from long before this; that is, he had been perfectly formed, he had grown through the stages by which his species evolved and had become a complete small Whale, with every organ laid down, when he was only 12 inches long. At that period in his fetal life when most unborn mammals look more like oysters than the adults they eventually become, the

I

Whale had his slender head, tiny flippers, and slim body tapering to the paired flukes of his tail: a perfect whale but in miniature soon after he was conceived—a precocious development it seemed, a mystery even to scientists. All he did from then on was to acquire his enormous size.

In his entire body, finally, the Whale felt a lack. More of something was needed. His mother's blood still came down the umbilical cord. Sped by the pulse of his infant heart, it flowed through his veins; but the blood was no longer satisfying. There was not enough oxygen in it. This emergency was felt by all mammal babies, including the human, when they had grown to the point where they could begin life on their own. And so the Whale did what the others did: in his discomfort he squirmed. His flippers and flukes, which would be floppy and limp until he was born, nevertheless tried to thrash about, and his body turned this way and that. *Help!* his motions were saying, and his mother's muscles were hearing that cry. The walls of his nest, until then so quiet, started to pulse and squeeze. Something was going to happen now.

The nest had produced an opening. It was not large enough, but the infant's own movements and a push by his mother were able to get him through. Next he found himself in a slippery tunnel. The infant himself was such a smooth shape that he should have slid out of it easily. All that was needed was to have his mother's squeeze-push continue. But it didn't, it stopped! This was not right and with the confining tightness here, the Whale could not make his misery known by expressive motions. Motion was the language of whales, all through their

2

lives, but the pressure on every side of him made the infant mute.

At the instant the Whale left her body, his mother would have to be near the surface, for he would need air at once. But the sea just then was a chaos of towering waves plunging over into the seething foam of the troughs. And how would a just-born infant be able to time his breaths so that he took only air into his blow-holes, not the tumbling and swirling waters? His mother was staying just under the waves' crashing fall, for now that the birth had commenced she might not be able to hold it back. But if she could she would delay it. And so the infant was finding himself immobilized in the narrow channel.

For the first time he was hearing clearly the sounds from outside his mother. Until then few had penetrated through her thick, insulating blubber. Sounds surround-ing him had been only those of his mother's living. Very loud was the *lub-dupp, lub-dupp* of her half-ton heart. Never ceasing, the beat was a lullaby, soothing, an assur-ance that everything was all right. Already his ears, were many times more acute than a human being's; he could also hear the blood rushing along in his mother's veins and arteries. These were sizable streams, some of her arteries being so large that a human child could have crawled through them; and her mighty heart pumped the blood along with enough force to send it quickly down her 96-foot length. Her other organs were doing their work, most of them quietly; no digestion was proceeding because this was the fasting half of her year. The infant could feel her muscles' thrust as she swam about, but the muscles were nearly silent.

3

Now having progressed almost to his exit, the Whale was hearing the outside sounds of his world-to-come. They warned of violence and peril. From above came crescendos of crashes, heard on all sides but loudest when a wave broke just over him and his mother. A towering storm was raging up there. Lines of waves were gnashing their way ahead, each one gathering itself from below, soaring and then hurling itself down in a long continuous cataract. These were the first sounds that greeted the Whale while he was being born, but to him they were only a great confusion.

The birth would have to take place; there was no turning back and no further waiting was possible. With the squeeze-push resumed behind him, the Whale reached the end of the tube. It was smallest there but it spread apart suddenly and he was out.

Oh, out! Nothing whatever pressing upon him, nothing surrounding him with protecting walls either! On all sides was a vast noisiness, swing of water, and a pounding down from above. The Whale's mother, having no teeth to bite the umbilical cord in two, made a quick jerk to break it and with the same motion swung under him, lifting him up and out of the sea. Into a nothingness: air! Oxygen! He gasped and took it into his lungs—this that he had been wanting so urgently. More of it, more! But a great wave came down on the two of them. The Whale sensed its fall and closed his blowholes, but water got into them. Instinct would tell him how he could force it out, though not yet. For his mother had sunk away under him, taking him with her below the surface, out of the foam and spray and the battering weight of the waves—too soon, but he couldn't stay out

4

up there, just breathing as he so needed to do, because of the oncoming ridges of water.

Their weight could flatten a newborn whale. His mother must lower him to a safer level, but up they went again into a trough between the waves' breaking . . . and down . . . and up, sometimes nearly caught by the waterfall. Oh, this was terrible weather in which to be born!

It was. His mother would never have chosen the height of a storm to introduce her whale baby to life. But here near the Tropics ferocious gales did arise suddenly. Within minutes, it seemed, screaming winds would come over the placid sea, driving the water up into mountainous combers, sending the spindrift flying and worst, slamming down with a crushing force on an infant that needed a quietly rocking cradle of gentle swells. A storm like this was the most dangerous time for a birth, but one never knew when the wind would come in like a ramming enemy. Anyway here the Whale was, born into this turmoil. One could say, though, that it was not an unsuitable welcome, for he belonged to the species of mightiest animals ever to live on earth.

Even below the surface the sea's rolling and tossing frequently pitched the Whale off his mother's back. There was little that he could do then but flounder about. His flippers and flukes, so flabby before he was born, had stiffened immediately; therefore now, when the water threw him around, in his fumbling way he was fighting it. During his very first moments of life he was trying to cope, not successfully but he robustly tried—he was that kind of whale.

The storm lasted too long. Thunder seemed to be splitting the sky wide open. Lightning was streaking out

of it, and torrential rain, a new hazard, for the Whale
didn't know yet how to turn on his side when he spouted.
His blowholes opened directly into the deluge, and each
time he breathed he took in some water. But he did sense
that he could blow it out when he had a chance. Nevertheless he was a very young baby, with muscles and
nerves quickly tiring, and after an hour of being pounded
and flung about he was exhausted and made only the
feeblest efforts to blow. His flippers and flukes had gone
limp again; they were just letting the water swing them.
His heart was still beating but with only a small weak
flutter. Soon he could be a lost whale.

As the wind and the thunder and lightning went on
to savage the farther seas, the Whale's mother, supporting him, kept him up in the air. She sensed that her
infant's body was now inert. If he had been dead she
would have known; since he wasn't, yet, how could she
quicken the life in him, how get his flippers to grasp her
sides, for he was making no effort to stay on her back?
When he started to slide away, she righted him and began swimming, letting him feel the strength of her muscles under him. Nothing helped, and so then, in her
fatalistic wild way, she just waited, still holding him out
of the gradually diminishing waves.

In the storm's terrible assault many whale infants
probably would have relaxed their hold on the cord that
tied them to life. The Whale didn't. A moment came
when somewhere below thought, below consciousness,
he might have been glad to loosen his grasp; when, even,
it might have seemed the right thing to do: *Let go now.*
And yet he held on. With all his tiny strength he would
cling to his life until it was snatched away.

At last, through her back, his mother could feel that he was reviving: the next time he took a breath his chest was deflated suddenly with his blow and then filled out again with new oxygen.

The waves were no longer cascading over. They would advance, roll under the whales, lift them, hold them high, start to pass beyond, let them down in a trough while the next wave advanced, rolled under them. . . . The sea was flattening gradually, the great clouds blew away and the sun came out.

The Whale still was not comfortable. Something new, a different lack, was making him restless. It was a need almost as strong as his hunger for oxygen several hours earlier, and his mouth moved across the back of his mother's head, groping.

She understood and, turning over, slid forward to bring his mouth to the pair of folds on her lower belly. These now spread apart and two immense nipples sprang out. The Whale had no means of sucking, but he closed his large inflatable tongue around one of the nipples, forming the tongue into a funnel with the small end in his throat. And at once, with strong pulses, his mother's breast muscles squeezed a great stream of milk—gallons of it—into him. It was ten times as rich as a cow's milk.

After he'd had enough his mother put one of her flippers under his chin so he wouldn't sink, and both of them lightly slept. At that time, late June, so much oil was contained in her blubber, which was nearly 12 inches thick, that she was a naturally floating object. She had recently finished six months of intensive feeding in the

Antarctic where, and only where, the food of southern blue whales could be found. By now, in the antarctic winter, the ice of those seas would have covered the food —but no matter. Her blubber had stored enough nourishment for herself and her young one until the next feeding season would open. During the six months between now and then she would gradually lose weight and buoyancy while her son would be gaining both and would become ever better able to stay on the surface effortlessly. Soon he would be gaining 200 pounds a day and every six and a half days would be a foot longer. Right now on his day of birth he was 24 feet in length and weighed over two tons—4400 pounds. No other infants who ever had lived were as large as blue whales; the adults into which they grew were the all-time giants. But the Whale did not think of his mother as being unique in the earth's history. She was just the right size, a dependable and concerned protector.

The next morning she disappeared—or seemed to; she was not far away. Sudden fright made him splash around helplessly. He was sinking! But no; by lifting his flukes, the large flaps shaped like butterfly wings at the end of his body, he found he could raise his head out of the surface. As his tail lifted and bent up his head, he had gone forward a little—the tail also had thrust. This small emergency was his first lesson in mastery of his element. When he felt that the water was rising along the sides of his head, he tried the maneuver again: he definitely did know how to keep his blowholes out of the surface.

His flukes had no muscles in them, they were not much more than envelopes of skin filled with fibers, now firm, but the hinder part of his body was really a tail, with strong muscles to raise and lower it, and the tail wagged the flukes, partly for extra push and as well to serve as a rudder. That second day he discovered too that depressing his tail sent him *down*. He would not be afraid to do that before very long, especially since he knew how to come up again.

He also was finding out what his flippers, those arm-like paddles, were for. They balanced him and prevented his rolling sideward unless he wanted to. What a wonderful body: it could turn in any direction, in this lovely supporting water where he would become almost weightless. How splendid to be a blue whale! Hints of future delights came to the infant while he was discovering what he could do.

More milk! Where was his mother? She was right there. When the folds in her flesh were open, the Whale, failing to grasp a nipple firmly, found himself under a rain of milk, which had spurted up six feet into the air! Next time he took her teat more precisely.

To bear this infant the mother had come to a large bay south of Africa's western shoulder—here because these waters were close to her own warm temperature and small whales needed that external heat. The blue whales that gathered in the Antarctic for summer feeding all came up into subtropical latitudes for the alternate season, for mating one year and birth of a young one the next. And two to four months of each year were spent in migrating between the two areas. This part of the ocean where the small Whale had been born was his mother's home place. She always returned here and knew it well —from the contours of the seabed and flow of the currents.

The storm had been only a brief disturbance and a more congenial world for the temperament of an infant whale followed. The sea lay quiet under a fresh cool breeze, the surface brushed into only the smallest of sun-splashed ripples, which flowed along the Whale's sides in a playful way.

He was enjoying all this when he felt his mother rise under him, lifting him so that he rode on her back. For a short time they went along at the top of the water and then she dipped below, not far but the infant must hold his breath till she rose into the air again; and then down, a little deeper and going faster and making some shallow turns. The Whale could feel her strong muscles working under him and their motions had as much meaning as spoken words: *You try this*—as soon he was doing, waving his tail up and down as she did but not balancing with his flipper-arms because those were holding onto her tight. When he grew tired from the exercise and too from excitement, she knew and returned with him to the surface where he nursed. And then they lay resting, the Whale's mother no doubt making him feel how pleased she was by his infant self.

During his first independent swim the Whale encircled her as she was idling on top of the water. What he learned on that day was not only what she was like but how he would look when he was grown, though at the time her immense size was just reassurance: she was a great fortress of a mother.

He found that her length was four times his, and she had a head ten feet wide. Being dark blue, she lay on the sea like the shadow of a cloud. Her skin was all glossy smooth, though with a few gray circular scars; the Whale would learn about those when he acquired some himself. She was perfectly streamlined. Her intimate organs were enclosed in those folds on her belly, and no visible ears showed on the sides of her head—tiny holes were all, even though she had phenomenal hearing, as the Whale also had. Her head tapered up to her shoulders and then only very gradually down to her tail. She was the sleekest of whales, wherefore she was one of the best swimmers —unlike the humpbacks, who were shaped somewhat like tadpoles, or the sperm whales that breasted the waves with huge cubical heads, seven feet high, wide, and deep, as the infant would see before long. His mother could swim up to 28 miles an hour in an emergency, but most of the others not half as fast.

At the height of the storm no one could tell which was a blown spout from the lungs of a whale and which was spray off the tops of waves; the air was everywhere full of mist. But after the winds calmed down the infant could see what a proud tall fountain was made by his mother's breath. Although coming from two blowholes, close together, the spout rose in a single jet, straight and strong, 20 to 30 feet high. Sadly it would always make her a conspicuous target for anyone wishing to kill a whale. Here in the warm air near the Equator the spout was not steamy, as it would be among the ice of the Antarctic, but was composed of droplets of oil, oil continually gathering in her lungs, as in his, with the life saving effect that the oil absorbed nitrogen, which would be formed in a whale's blood during dives, and the oil, dispersed in spouts, would prevent the bubbles that can be fatal to human divers.

This was only one of several almost miraculous

adaptations that allowed whales to live in the sea. They had once been land animals, browsing among the giant ferns and evergreen trees of 40 million years ago; they still had—the young Whale himself had—useless leg bones for walking which were now buried in flippers and flanks. At first the whales could not have survived a dive of half a mile down, but they had developed this oily foam in their lungs, which they did, however, have to get rid of frequently. It was fortunate when the Whale's mother timed her spouts to come after his; otherwise he would gasp in her oily spray and carbon dioxide, the exhausted vapor from a body almost 100 feet long—polluted air until breezes drove it away.

Of all that a bright young whale soon might observe, one fact was overwhelmingly important: none of these others around him had to keep constantly going up to the surface to breathe. All the fishes, even the sharks got their oxygen from the water itself; all had gills, those ruffles along the sides of their throats which drew water in and out and extracted oxygen from it. Why didn't the Whale have them? Almost 300 times every 24 hours, day and night, forever, he would have to come back into the atmosphere of the land animals among whom his ancestors once had lived. Was he still, basically, one of them? Was dry land, even now, his true home? If not why, in 40 million years, had evolution not provided him with a breathing apparatus to make life in the water more practical? While other air-breathing animals could forget their need for a constant supply of oxygen—their lungs sucked it in with unconscious regularity—the Whale would always have to make a voluntary effort to fill his lungs.

There would surely be times when the need to rise

to the surface every five minutes would seem a hardship
—except that his movement in water, even swimming up
to the top for air, was so strong and supple. The Whale,
like his mother and all other blues, had a brain with an
extra development of the poise and balancing structure,
the cerebellum, and so they could manage their huge
bodies with silken refinement. It was surely a satisfaction
to express such a talent. And being able to bend in three
dimensions, which a fish could not do, and very nearly
able to ignore gravity, as birds could not, probably made
the Whale more physically free than any other creature
alive.

He soon showed signs that he would become an
excellent swimmer. And he had another skill to perfect:
his means of avoiding collisions. He was sharing the sea
with countless neighbors, all of them, too, swimming
about; indeed if the dry-land world were as fully popu-
lated as oceans were, the air would be densely swarming
with birds, insects, bats and other mammals like flying
squirrels. Marine creatures had to be very adept at weaving their way through the paths of so many others and
when they were first born they had to learn how to do
that, as did the Whale.

The great problem was that most of the water was
turbid, especially here off the coast of Africa where the
Congo River was releasing its load of silt, or in any part
of the ocean blurred by clouds of plankton, "the dust of
living specks." The Whale's eyes were blue, the ocean's
color, and they looked out with a certain knowing expression, seemingly conscious; but they were small in
comparison with his size—they would never be larger
than grapefruit. And they lacked the cones that would

show him color. He never would see the changing hues in the sky and the reflection of these on the water, never the sunrise, the lofty dome of noon, or the splendor of the sun's last light. The Whale would see them but only as grades of pearly radiance.

In the water eyes alone would not allow him to swim about swiftly for danger of hitting other undersea creatures or, later, the seabed and its rocks and ridges; his element would never be one to know visually. Out in the air he could not see a distance more than twice the length of his mother. Under the surface his eyes were more efficient but they were hindered because half the sun's light was lost at a depth of six feet in a sea like this. In his first days of swimming alone, even then in his newborn size, he was so large that those who had better eyes would spray out of his path as he drew near—except the octopuses and their near relatives, squids, which swam backward and couldn't see where they were going. A few times they bumped into *him,* when, alarmed, they would squirt out a cloud of ink in which to hide or escape—a small patch of total night in the ocean.

Lower down it was night everywhere, but the Whale knew that he was among living beings because of the many sounds: fish drumming on their air bladders, tapping their teeth, croaking, squealing, chirping, singing. These and other voices pricked the Whale's interest and he soon discovered how he could know much more about the creatures there in the dark.

Whenever he rode on his mother's back and they went below to the level where eyes were of little use, she kept sending out probing clicks, small stabs of sound. Was she warning the others that whales were coming?

The young one himself was listening to her clicks, which were pitched very high. For that reason those sounds did not spread out in all directions, as sounds in the human range do. Because they went forth at so many cycles a second they could be focused like arrows, precisely aimed. The Whale came to recognize that his mother was feeling ahead with them and then he became aware that the clicks returned echoes from whatever they hit. The echoes were telling the whales that they were approaching something, and by shifting her target about, the mother could learn how large it was; and if it was moving, how fast and in what direction. And by the length of time it took for the return of the echoes she also knew how far away it was. If the object was stationary, maybe a dreaming fish, as she came closer she would investigate with faster clicks. This ear view was actually more clear in deep water than even the sharpest eyes could have shown, because the clicks and their echoes could penetrate roiliness and the dark. And when the young Whale began to grasp what his mother was doing the whole sea came alive for him. He too began to listen for echoes and even could start to interpret them.

It was a special day then as the Whale's mother, with him on her back, was swimming along at a medium level when the Whale felt a swish on his face and, wanting to learn what was causing it, made some clicks of his own. He had not known that he could! It had happened involuntarily and when an echo returned he clicked again and again. He didn't learn what was there because his clicks were not aimed with skill, but having found he could do this, he spent more and more time where there was partial light and he could both see and hear. That was

16

not a deliberate project, rather was due to the fact that the Whale was still timid about going alone into the blacker depths; but the effect was to match the evidence gained with his eyes and that with his ears and meanwhile have practice in targeting.

He, like most young blues, had a lively interest in everything new, a bright curiosity that would get him into trouble sometimes but also would give him much pleasure. And what a quickening world he had entered, both below and above the surface a world ever changing, diverting, bringing into his days a succession of strangers and mysterious voices, unpredictable weather, light, and movement of water, a world always different and usually harmonious.

Being the largest animal there and eventually the strongest, with the power of 47 horses, it would seem that he must be entirely safe. He was not. A blue whale had several natural enemies, two during his youth and another who might attack when he was of any age. And besides these dangers there was the adversary, man.

As everywhere, some animals in the sea were eaten by other animals—a sad thought but not one to cause despair about nature's program since the deaths were only a way to insure continuing life. It was not until the arrival of men that living creatures were turned into *things,* trivial, insignificant things like machine oil and car wax and shoe polish. In the making of all such products there were inanimate substitutes for the bodies of whales. And the killing of sensate beings, especially intelligent beings, to provide nonessential materials seemed to justify more profound disillusionment than nature's allowing one life to be transformed as food into another life.

Men had the disadvantage of pygmy size but the huge benefit of inventiveness. Any blue whale, then, would need to outwit human technology. But could he? Was there any way that a whale could win such a mismatched conflict?

In any case the young Whale would have an animal's acceptance of the inevitable and would carry on in the ways typical of his kind since long before men had evolved. He would be great in size and also great in his consideration for other creatures and in helpfulness, as when he would hold a sick or injured comrade up at the surface to breathe. The Whale himself would live with no visible sign of bitterness. As his limber body would make its excursions in the supporting and yielding water, that beautiful swimming would be his play and perhaps his delight, since his motions would have more subtlety than even the finest flyers' among the birds, reaching its climax when he would mate and his grace would interweave with another's.

When he could avoid the new hideous hazards he would be one of the most fortunate animals on the earth. If he could write his autobiography that is possibly what he would say—at least in the beginning.

2

Everything Else Was Small

In the early days of his life the Whale spent most of his time at the surface—for its essential air and also because more things were happening there. He could see and hear lively splashes and chases. Dorados were leaping out of the water, always coming down flat on their sides, noisily smacking up bursts of spray. They did that for fun, but when flying fish were about, sailing up into the air and away, the dorados tore after them at the top of the water, trying to be on the spot where a flyer would have to come down. Flying fish were their favorite food, and with many dorados here, more than 40 to share them, they all went after the flying fish savagely.

The dorados, sometimes called "sailors' dolphins," were not the small whales now known to most men as dolphins; they were true fish *(Coryphaena)* and were said to be the most beautiful in the sea. It was not because of their shape that they were admired, for their heads and necks were so large that they seemed grotesque. A four-foot dorado could have a head 12 inches high, perhaps a deterrent to getting up speed, for in chasing a flying fish the dorado swam with his forehead out of the surface. The fame of its beauty was due to something the Whale could not see—its rainbow colors, quick-changing, washing over its scales in a display that was always most dazzling during its death. At men's banquets in Pompeii dorados were sometimes killed at the table to give guests the pleasure of seeing the fires of their dying. But in life too the dorados would blush and go pale in pink, green, yellow and blue, and though the Whale could not see these hues they were visible to him as waves of shine.

The Whale was entertained by the dorados, and as much by the flying fish. They left the water by giving a mighty thrust with the lower blades of their tails, which flung them up into the air where their breast fins opened like wings and carried them 200 yards or more . . . beyond the Whale's sight, but often one ended its glide nearby and the Whale could see how, at the instant it touched the water, another lunge with its tail again sent it up, not so far this time and once more a dip until all its momentum was gone. Especially on sunny days when a lively breeze helped to sustain their flight, the air seemed to be full of the bright little fish, looking as if the waves' sparkles had taken wing. The Whale, stimulated and starting to have some playful urges himself, would make a quick vertical dive down to shivery depths and then dash for the surface, as he came out of it lobbing down hard with his tail—he too could make a fine splash, bigger than any dorado's!

Now what could this possibly be, floating along with the current? It lay near the top of the water, a disc on edge—nine feet wide. Alive? It was not shiny, it had no scales, but on each of two sides it had an appendage that looked like a flipper, narrow and longer than the Whale's infant flippers. The Whale would investigate. He swam close to the object, which made no move. It was just drifting. With his snout the Whale touched the end of the lower appendage.

Splash! The fish—for that's what it was, an ocean sunfish, or headfish *(Mola)*—sprang forward. It had been idling along, soaking up the bright morning's warmth, but now it swam quickly away and was indeed a curious sight. It had no tail, just a slight skirt of ruffled fin from the top to bottom of its rear end, and only those two thin fins, one standing up from its back and the other descending below its belly. To go ahead it was twisting the fins with a sculling motion, surely the strangest swimming arrangement of any fish here, when the usual fish way to progress was by a side-to-side fanning of upright tails— or in the case of a whale, fanning one's tail up and down. And this fish appeared monstrously large, for it weighed a ton. The Whale didn't follow it. Who could tell what damage its mouth with two overlapping teeth, like a beak, might do? (Various jellyfishes, crustaceans, and other marine creatures could have told what damage if they had not already been in the sunfish's stomach.)

It seemed a lazy fish, or perhaps was a female and tired from a recent feat of shedding her eggs in the ocean, of which she laid 300 million at any one time.

The whale's eyes and clicks told him that his fish neighbors were of every size up to that of the giant sunfish. There were schools of tiny ones staying so close together it seemed that the many were one single creature . . . now streaming ahead, now drawing together, a mass of circling bits, a flickering image. Almost all living things in the sea moved continually, as the Whale and his mother did. The water's restlessness was born in them.

Fish in general seemed to be shaped much like himself and his mother. But octopuses and squids were like bags with arms waving out of the tops; and just below the arms, eyes. The bags moved by jet propulsion, taking in seawater and squirting it out to send them along in straight lines very fast—backward, so that even though the creatures had excellent eyes they sometimes hit what was behind them. Very strange was a fish that would blow itself up like a big ball with spines all over it—a porcupine fish. And something puzzling indeed: whether the Whale was up in the water's visual layer or down below, a school of little striped fish swam ahead of him. Why? And how did they know which way he would go? Perhaps they thought they were guiding him. Men called them pilot fish but the Whale certainly knew that he was not following them—or was he? Besides all of these there were other shadowy figures whose blurred outlines approached and then moved away. Many creatures; and there was a wonderful harmony in their flowing about, each of them passing in and out through the companies of his neighbors, going forward or giving way without argument, winding among lives all in motion, most of them with a lovely grace.

With his clicks and echoes the Whale could sense the smooth turnings around him, but there was one fascinating way that his eyes were more useful in even the depths, in fact the darker the better: for eyes could pick up lights, which no ear could do. His ears could not find the millions of tiny animals of the plankton that had luminous spots on their bodies. They were like miniature fireflies, a few of them shining continuously but more that blazed with excitement whenever one of the larger creatures brushed by. They could turn on their lights at will and when some of them brightened, many others would also flash their small beams, kindling together what appeared to be sparks, glowing embers, and sheets of flame in the sea.

It was not an impressive show in the daytime, but at night when the water became black dark, everything moving trailed streamers of light. The Whale's mother did and, being so large, she illuminated the whole sea around her. She was a conflagration compared with the small bright streaks that followed a passing bream or bonito. To those fish and most others the young Whale himself looked immense, defined as he was by pennants of fire.

Why did the plankters light up, for whose benefit were they flaring? For one another no doubt, to warn, attract, be identified or simply to be in touch. Most of the animals in the plankton had eyes and probably recognized their own fellows by the patterns of lights on their bodies. The plankters could not have had any conception of what a whole whale looked like, nor did they see a man as a man, though when one in a boat dropped something over the side, the plankters would flash over a much wider area. Or if the man shone one of his own big lamps on the water, a brightness would spread as if many plankters were answering.

To a human observer the living illumination was always impressive, but there was a greater marvel known only to those with microscopes. Seen under a lens the plankters' lights were of all colors—nearly every observer described them as flashing jewels—and the lights always harmonized with the tints of the owners' bodies: pink, violet, blue, silver-green, scarlet, orange. But after the human eyes became used to the dazzling display, it was the forms of the tiny structures that seemed most amazing.

Some had an exquisite beauty: the radiolarians, for example, which were balls of glass (silicon) pierced in elegant lacy designs and with delicate little antennae, the whole looking like tiny spaceships designed for artistic effect rather than technological traveling. Just visible to a good eye were sapphirinas, minute creatures over which rainbow hues flashed in waves, as over the big dorados; copepods resembling insects, gnat-size but with tails that a peacock might envy; Venus's girdles, long, flat and transparent, edged with bright iridescence; snails with butterfly wings and luminous jellyfish. Those called comb jellies suggested gooseberries, striped with combs which had mobile teeth, a means of moving about; and glass arrowworms had sharp black eyes that could look in every direction, including inside themselves, for what narcissistic purpose one wondered. Some men who thought that surrealistic designs were amusing when made by themselves were a little uncomfortable when confronted by living animals that seemed even less rational. They tried to see the small bodies as like things in the human world: anchors, stars, flowers, seeds borne on thistledown, children's tops, lances. Those descriptions were far-fetched however. In human terms most of the plankton animals looked so nonsensical only one who was daft, it seemed, could have designed them. One observer said the siphonophores, *Physophora hydrostatica*, looked like renditions in glass of jazz solos.

With extraordinary small mobile hairs and other contrivances the plankton animals in the Whale's ocean were migrating many feet up and down every day. They came up in the evenings, fed most of the night on the floating plankton plants that the daytime sun had encouraged to grow; and then as dawn approached, the tiny creatures went back down to the lower levels. But sometimes an individual or a group would linger behind the others; that is, they were not being pushed up and down by some automated force—they had their own way of doing things. And even those that didn't go all the way to the surface usually moved on a vertical course each day. While some were traveling between the top of the water and 200 feet down, others were rising from 600 feet below the surface to 200 feet. Why? Men thought that it was because the various layers of water are often flowing in different directions, and so a change of depth gave the plankters a ride to a new location and maybe to richer foods. Or did they just like mobility? Men seemed unable to imagine any other reason for their moving about than for better nourishment.

A man in a boat off the coast of Guernsey, one of the British Channel islands, or off the coast of California on the other side of the world, puts his hand down in the water, spreads his fingers and moves them back and forth slowly. Between the fingers flow small streams of light. "Phosphorescence," he says and by naming the light diminishes its significance. For phosphorescence isn't composed of one substance, like the phosphorus put in fertilizers. It's a community of living, seeking, responding, flashing little beings, most of them made, literally, of colored glass. The Whale, too, failed to see them as neighbors. They were most important to him as the glow surrounding his mother.

She was not always with him, for she belonged to a species understood to be wanderers and as long as she knew where her infant was by her echo clicks, she would relieve her restlessness by circling about over the area that was her summer home place. It had been chosen ten years before by her and her permanent mate; here in one year she would conceive an offspring and here the next year would bear him—a routine of interludes between their migrations down to the antarctic feeding grounds. As long as her mate was with her it had been an unquestioned habit that they would return to this summer sea; and this year, although she was alone, again it was to here that she had come back.

"Here" was the surface above three small submerged mountain peaks, easy to recognize by a whale's sonar system. The peaks stood at the end of an undersea canyon, a gorge formed by the outflow of Africa's Congo River. The banks of the canyon provided another landmark, and up at the top two familiar currents flowed past. Both currents were swinging westward, side by side but easy to tell apart because one was warm, almost hot, and the other quite cold. Men called the warm one, on the north side of the canyon, the Equatorial Countercurrent because it flowed from the mid-Atlantic doldrums east to Africa where the coast turned it around toward the mid-Atlantic again. It brought the high temperatures of the equatorial region and also a remnant flavor of the Sargasso Sea, of the weeds and the eels that bred there, and some of the human pollution becalmed in that windless area. The Whale's mother, without understanding what caused the flavor, could distinguish it by the taste buds on the back of her tongue.

The other, the cold current, also came from the west and was reversed by the African coast. Called the Benguela Current, it originated in the Antarctic, flowed eastward until it reached the immovable African continent and there, after turning northward along the continent for a way, came as far as the Congo River where it met and was deflected by the Equatorial Countercurrent and had to swing westward, also out toward the mid-Atlantic. Although she had borne her son in the warmer one, the mother, from time to time, made a little foray into the cool, bracing Benguela Current, perhaps because it reminded her of the ice fields around the whales' feeding grounds where, after a few more months, there would come an end to this summer's fasting. The Benguela

Current didn't have any particular taste except for the sediment it had scoured off the African shore. It was the less salty current, having been fed by several landward rivers, whereas the current from the Sargasso Sea came from one of the saltiest waters on earth.

The two contrasting flows were along the top of the ocean. Below them there was a southbound layer of water and on the seabed a northward creep of very cold water indeed. The whales wouldn't go all the way down into the lowest one unless they were making very deep dives. That was something the mother and son had to do before long, since it was necessary for him to practice every kind of a whale's swimming.

It was on one of her brief absences in the Benguela Current that she heard a scream from her son—one of fright and perhaps of pain. Instantly she sped toward him.

He had been enjoying himself that day. As always his curiosity inspired him to investigate anything that seemed new and interesting. He was tuned for excitement and his ears scanned the waters around him. What was that? He could hear a prolonged splashing. He listened. The sound came from farther away than the Whale ever had gone alone, but he hurried toward it. As it grew louder he could recognize two kinds of disturbance. The lighter kind was continuous and then there was another, intermittent *bash . . . bash . . . bash,* all the commotion being up at the surface.

When he came near the Whale saw what was happening. A big brown thresher-shark was encircling a school of mackerel, driving them into a closer mass by swimming around and around them and beating the water by slashing into it with a very long pointed tail. The upper lobe of the tail was the same length as the shark's body, ten feet. Like a flail it was, and it whipped into the water in a way that was terrifying the mackerel, now a company of giddily desperate fish.

The Whale, sensing slaughter to come, was mesmerized. The shark would make one more swing around the prey before it attacked them. But—hideous! The shark, catching the scent of the Whale, streaked away from the fish toward the infant! As he flung about to escape, the Whale screamed for his mother. A shriek it was, for the shark's teeth had fastened into his side!

They had ripped out a large bite. Dazzled with pain the Whale sped away. Frantically he was pumping his infant tail, staying up at the surface where the water's resistance was least. *Where was his mother?* Faster, oh, faster! For he could hear the splash of the shark coming on, gaining behind him.

The shark had lost a few seconds in his pursuit because he had not expected a very young whale to dash away so decisively. More often they thrashed about in confused panic. But this time the bite had been deep and its white-hot stab had sent the Whale headlong.

The shark, having swallowed one mouthful of the sweet mammal flesh, was determined to have another—many more! His snout had come even with the Whale's fibrous flukes. No treat, those, not when six or eight feet ahead was the victim's flank, juicy and trailing provocative blood. The shark's fin was grazing the skin of the Whale and the lofty blade of his thresher tail was flashing into the view of the Whale's right eye. Now breathless and with his energy draining away, the young one put all his remaining strength into a last burst of speed. The hunter's mouth reached his side, opened to clamp again into the living meat when the shark exploded suddenly into scattered lumps of its flesh. For the Whale's mother had rammed it with a force that had killed it instantly, the water here within seconds becoming rank with shattered bones, bloody flesh and half-digested mackerel.

Quickly the Whale's mother slipped under him and carried him back to the home waters where she surfaced to comfort the infant with warm gallons of milk, afterward stroking his wound lightly, tenderly, with her flipper. While he was close to her no other shark would attack, but they must leave this familiar place as soon as the infant's panic was quieted, for the blood in the sea would summon more of these enemies and no infant whale would be safe except in a parent's near and protective presence.

It had been a rare thing for a blue whale to attack. The mother had no proper weapons, no teeth to bite, no claws to rend, but she did have her speed, 41 feet a second when necessary, and her immense size and strength. She would not use these advantages except in an emergency, but then she would hurl herself headfirst at the enemy, and that defense, in the case of a shark, would be enough. There might be occasions when this form of attack could not be used, but this time it had been adequate.

After he finished nursing the young one lay at his mother's side, becoming gradually reassured. The wound would heal.

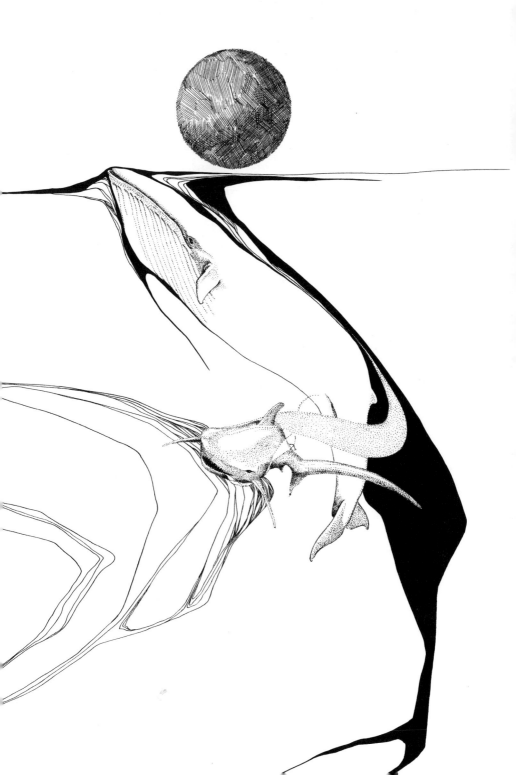

South of the home place there was a large sink in the seabed, called by men the Angola Basin. Water three miles deep was above it, which made the Basin a good part of the sea for young whales to learn depth diving. In the case of her four other offspring the whale mother had led them there as soon as they started away on their southward migration, but this time, because her infant was wounded, she turned instead toward the coast.

In almost every whale species there was an impulse to go near a shore whenever in trouble—ill or injured. That tendency puzzled men. Why, when one of the greatest hazards to whales was the chance of stranding on beaches, did they deliberately put themselves into this danger at the times when they were least fit? Was there some comfort in being in shallower water? There it was sometimes warmer, and was that the reason they fled toward the land? It didn't have any of the signs of a practical or a learned reaction. In fact their headlong flight shoreward more often suggested panic.

How many, if any, stranded whales that had died in that way had come there with some sort of purpose? Lacking a storm tide to rescue them, stranding was always fatal. Whales did not have a land animal's type of temperature control; out in the air in a sunny atmosphere a whale overheated and died of what essentially was a fever. And yet they did come. It is not necessary, nor possibly reasonable, to think of their motive as a kind of suicide impulse, somewhat as land animals often go off alone when they sense that death is approaching. But in view of the mystery one might wonder whether some very deep instinct draws them toward what, millions of years ago, was their home. Does the land still seem a refuge in spite of all the whales' marine adaptations and long experience? Do the kelp and other seaweeds found only in shallower waters remind them of great terrestrial plants, trees and tall ferns, under which they once foraged? If any such influence sends them toward the land in emergencies, the whales would not, of course, know of it consciously, and these speculations may be too far-fetched to be taken seriously; perhaps their panic flight toward the land must remain unexplained.

Not actually near the beach but in sight of land if they had had better eyes, the mother and son idled slowly along the coast while his bite was healing. There were some unfamiliar small organisms to watch, freshwater fish and crustaceans that had wandered out from the Congo River into this salty element where they would not long survive. That very salt, however, would help speed the Whale's recovery. And so the day came before very long when the Whale's side was well again, and his energy proved that the motions of swimming had ceased to hurt. His interest and curiosity returned and soon led him and his mother into a small and pleasant adventure.

The two were leisurely going along, not far from the African town of Luanda, when the Whale's revived curiosity led him to dash away from her. For he had seen a strange object floating along the surface. Was it a fish? It didn't seem to be swimming and yet it progressed. He must know about this. He swam near it and standing on his tail boldly, he raised his head out of the water. It was a boat, the first he had seen. It had a sail, as large as one of his mother's tail flukes, and was nipping along over the ripples almost silently, the only sound being its whispering bow wave. But if this wasn't an animal there was an animal on it, one long and narrow and small, hardly a quarter as long as the infant Whale. A man. As the Whale came in closer, the man leaned over the side of the boat and made friendly sounds. An amazing thing: he had eyes and his eyes met the interested eye of the Whale and something happened between them, a feeling that passed from one to the other. The Whale, in his excitement at this, turned a somersault in the water. Then he came in still farther. The man splashed a handful of water at his face and the Whale would have laughed if he could.

His mother approached from behind with her great, easy strength. Staying back a few yards, she was watching cautiously to be sure that her infant was safe. She thought that he would be for she knew what these men were like. She had seen the small boats before and the men who sailed them. They did not catch whales, they were not killers. Men were of two kinds, it seemed—like whales. Just as there were safe whales and killer whales, so there were men who were harmless and others that killed. The killer men were usually in the Antarctic, where a whale mother and her infant would soon have to go—unfortunately, because that was the only place she knew that a blue-whale's food could be found. The men there also rode in boats, but very large ones with cruel-sounding machines. Better were tiny boats sailed by only one man, and the mother did not have any animosity toward them. She was too good-natured to feel anger toward all men just because some were killers—as soon dread all whales because there were killer whales.

One would think that the man on this day might have been afraid of her, for one brush of her flipper could have upset his boat. But he, for his part, knew these whales and understood that they managed their mammoth bodies in the most careful way. He was dark, even blacker than she was, and when he stood up and walked to the back of the boat, he moved with a natural sort of grace, like a whale's.

To the east there were palm trees along a low shoreline. The whales could not see that far, but the mother kept sending down solar signals which told her the seabed was rising beneath them. Soon she and her son must turn back, but they stayed with the boat as long as there was no danger of being stranded upon the beach. For this little incident was diverting—three creatures, all gentle, meeting, exchanging their interest in one another, all three, it might be, having their emotions warmed a little by contact with another so different. Two years later, on the other side of the ocean, the Whale would remember this occasion dimly and recognize that some men were not enemies, as he would have grown in the meantime to think of them.

3

Only the Harmless Can Play

The Whale had been born at the end of June. Since then two weeks had passed. In five and a half more months, at the end of November, he should be weaned and start feeding himself. Most young animals had to learn how to find and, in the case of carnivores, attack and kill what they eat. The food preferred by blue whales, the plankton euphausids or krill, would be so abundant where the Whale and his mother were going that he would need to do no more than open his mouth and they would crowd in. His mother knew where that fortunate concentration was: around South Georgia Island, east of Cape Horn and in the same icy-cold latitude. The island was several thousand miles from this African coast but the route was familiar to the Whale's mother and there was a purposeful steadiness in her swimming as she and her infant started away.

Ordinarily she was not so near land at this early stage of her annual journey. She had come here only because her son's wound had made her wish to be close to a shore. Now that he appeared to be well, they would go back into much deeper water. In all other years when she and her mate had set out from their summer sea, they had gone straight south into the Basin. There they had both enjoyed the greater buoyancy all that volume of water under them gave; and in alternate years, when an infant was with them, they had introduced him to the colder and darker depths. Beyond the Basin there would be no other place as good for a young one to learn depth diving. The Whale would need that skill when they would encounter killer men later. As they left the coast, then, he was starting into an important new phase of his growing up.

They hadn't gone far when the pulse of the passing waves began to carry a new and astonishing sound. Present everywhere, always, were the mumbling movements of waters stirred by the earth's turning and, when winds were whipping the surface, the crash of rollers and hiss of collapsing foam. These, the seas' impersonal protests, were too familiar to attract attention, but now there was something different: a voice clearly of flesh and blood and, remarkably, not calling but seeming a voice raised for the pure pleasure of making these sounds, which were expressive and musical, what men might describe, did describe, as a song.

The young Whale, hearing something so strange, slowed the beat of his tail. But then he sensed that his mother was not alarmed and he dashed ahead. He must investigate this, and his mother seemed willing to come along.

The singing was under water. The Whale couldn't hear it when he surfaced to blow or nurse but when he submerged the voice was clear and definite even though it was, in the beginning, more than ten miles away. As the Whale and his mother drew near he fell back to swim at her side and she slowed their pace, for—as she expected—a group of humpback whales were ahead and it was not the wild way to rush impulsively into a new situation.

Only one humpback was singing but he was using two voices, one a falsetto, the other a bass voice much lower. The upper voice sounded like that of a very young animal, even the Whale himself if he had been as articulate. It was light and thin, seeming youthfully flexible as it glided around in a high register, plaintive and softly shrill.

And then, as if answering, came low gruff tones that better expressed what the singer was: an animal large in size and weight—and a little impatient perhaps. For a time the two voices suggested a dialogue between an infant and parent.

On a new theme then the humpback began to sing in the baritone range of a human voice. There the singing sounded most musical. One often repeated phrase would slide upward and finish with three puffed staccatoes. There was also a fast staccato, all on the same note, that could almost have been the beat of an outboard motor. Somewhat more throaty were liquid gulping and gurgling tones, like water tumbling along over stones, and with those were quite resonant sounds, as if the stones faintly chimed. Single clear tones were as pure as those from a flute or horn, those, especially, bouncing back from the shallow seabed with echoes so real it was hard to tell which was the original voice. Usually the singer sent out those notes with pauses between them, and an echo would blend with the tone following in a very harmonious way. Finally, sometimes it seemed as if the humpback sang in a large, long tunnel where echoes themselves were echoing, so that the voices came from many directions and made the ocean sound very spacious.

There had been much variety in the humpback's song, splashes of sound that seemed as unplanned as images chasing one another through a whale's mind; and so the singing appeared to be random. Actually it wasn't. During the time the Whale and his mother were on the way coming, the musical themes had been repeated several times, which made them a real song and like nothing else the Whale ever had heard, or ever would hear, in the ocean.

Incidentally, the music that sailors used to think they heard in the hulls of their wooden boats probably was the singing of humpback whales. Most sounds cannot pass from water to air, or from air into water, but wood partly submerged will transmit through that sound barrier. Some primitive fishermen put their ears against the ends of their paddles and say they can hear the voices of fish below. The reason that divers can't hear the underwater sounds is that bubbles of air in their ears won't let the sounds pass.

Echo clicks told the two who approached that the singer had stationed himself a little apart from the rest of the humpbacks. There were ten or twelve of them. He was the first to sense that two blue whales were near, and he fell silent. The blue whales might have gone on then but there was plenty of other interest here. For all the humpbacks were moving about, not in any concerted way but with something like growing excitement: something, it seemed, was about to break into action. It did! As the Whale and his mother listened and watched, the others began a great splashing romp. They had immensely long flippers, white, which were bashing down on the water everywhere, almost concealing the frolicking whales in spray. But this didn't release all their exuberant spirits. They commenced leaping out of the water —entirely out, sometimes to cut an arc in the air and then smoothly, gracefully knife back into the waves, giving a flippant toss of their flukes as they disappeared. Then more and more of them chose to make high dives up into the sunny air and with a twist of their bodies, let themselves, the great expanse of their 40-foot length, fall flat on the surface. Their tremendous weight—30 tons for each whale—sent up geysers of water that rained back over a very wide area—on the Whale and his mother— with a crashing so loud that it was heard 25 miles away by the man in his little boat.

The humpbacks were breaching in every way possible to a whale, rolling out of the water, somersaulting, and again and again throwing themselves out completely and coming down on their backs or bellies. Then gradually all but two played less boisterously. They gave way to a pair whose game had been the most active and who were now slapping each other wildly but soon more tenderly, with short pauses then, to draw together until finally, lying face to face, they had a moment of obliterating all else in delight.

Not long after that the festivities came to an end and the humpbacks idled around or lay resting up at the surface. And the Whale and his mother left, to continue east on their way to the Angola Basin.

Except for his mother, the humpbacks had been the only whales the young one had seen. They were not even half her size but were nearly twice as large as himself— the first creatures to make him seem small. A little tired from the excitement of the humpbacks' display and also perhaps slightly subdued by this revelation of other whales' bigness, he swam forward beside his mother in a way docile for him. What he would not have recognized was that he had seen all that activity, that spectacular leaping, and had heard bewildering volumes of sound without even a tremor of fear. His world on this day had been truly a blue-whale's world, one without animosity. In a few months the humpbacks would have gone south to the Antarctic, to Australia where they too would grow fat on a diet of plankton. The song and the high leaping were not in a blue-whale's temperament, but in one important way blue whales and humpbacks were alike: both could enjoy themselves in easy, relaxed play because their kind of food did not require them to stalk and kill other mammals, creatures akin to themselves. A hunter must keep himself on the alert, ready to pounce. He can't let himself go in a good-natured mood that is not looking for victims but for a chance to have fun.

The Whale might have become a depth diver more quickly if he himself had not been so playful. He often swam at his mother's side, but not for long before he would suddenly somersault and if she turned back to find him, would make a chase of it. He loved chases, the kind that were only games. If his mother started away from him with some private intention, he sometimes would race ahead of her, or try to keep up behind her, nudging her flukes, meaning, *Catch me!* He never jumped all the way out of the water, as the clowning humpbacks did, but he splashed his mother by lobtailing when they were up at the surface; or he splashed with his flipper and once, very daring, he slapped her side as he was finishing nursing and then she whirled around and slapped him, but he ducked down in the water where slaps don't work, and that time she did chase him, which was the best ever.

So far she had not had much inclination to play with this little one as she had with her other infants, because she was depressed by the loss of her mate. But the determined Whale was arousing the playfulness in herself and she began to respond to his splashes and nudges. Besides their fun they were doing some intricate swimming together, first one then the other leading in weaving tumbles and rolls. It wouldn't be long now before this came closer to practice in diving deeply, but they were distracted one morning by seeing a different kind of frolic.

A spanking wind blew from the southeast and here, as if they were the living spirits of tossing waves, came a band of 80 or 90 dolphins *(Steno bredanensis),* at play

with the breakers and with each other. They were vaulting up out of the foaming crests, racing among themselves, proceeding in groups of six or eight that crossed and recrossed their lines of advance. The striking thing, aside from the dolphins' quick and vivacious movements, was that they seemed to be playing as teams. There was an obvious amiability in the whole company, but they divided into small ranks for maneuvers that 90 dolphins together could hardly manage. They turned their gambols into games and, whether or not the teams were competing (who could tell?), the whole object of progress through waves appeared to be lively sport. The humpbacks, except for the two who were mating, had seemed to leap and splash as they individually wished; blue whales frolicked as families, but the dolphins were playing as squads and meanwhile were chirping and calling to one another. The Whale and his mother had not submerged. The dolphins separated to pass around them, for the mother, nearly ten times their size, seemed as large as an island. They knew that she was no threat and for their part the dolphins would not inconvenience blue whales, just go by in their cheerful conviviality. If they had been hungry they might have stopped to eat squids, their favorite food, but squids were everywhere and so dolphins could spend most of their time in their jolly play. (If men had been there they might have called these dolphins the handsomest whales anywhere in the ocean, for they were gray above, white beneath, with the white and gray dappled across their chests against a background of delicate rose.)

Dolphins were not the only ones coming and going in the Angola Basin. Here the blue whales were in the shipping lane between Europe and South Africa, and the grind of the vessels' engines, transmitted through their reverberating steel hulls, filled the sea with metallic clatter. While a ship was passing the din made it harder to hear the delicate echoes from sonar clicks; and the ships' sounds were distressing in a more general way. They destroyed a little the right and comfortable naturalness of a whale's world. When men and men's inventions came into that world, they didn't fit into the flow of normal wild happenings. The ships' unchanging thrust was alien to blues' impulsiveness, and a whale had no intuitive way to adjust to it.

The ships were not always passing and when they weren't, the Whale could get on with learning to make a new kind of dive. His mother had no organized plan for teaching him—no compulsion to take him down at any particular time or in any particular way. Without consciously thinking about it, she would rely on his developing wish to try this new thing. He was as sure to grow into that stage as he was to keep putting on weight from her milk. Some day soon he would want to go far below with her, and when he did she would be with him to make sure that he didn't dive down too far or come up too fast; as events would unfold she would do everything necessary. Her sense of what would be needed and her willingness to carry it out could be depended upon. That was the way of an animal mother.

She herself liked to sound here because in other years echo clicks had told her that no obstructions were there below—no submerged mountain peaks, no canyons with high banks, nothing but a flat seabed so deep that a whale would be in no danger of reaching it. She would make a few dives for her own pleasure and those would be her infant's first lesson.

He would see how she emptied her lungs for this: with four or five short quick spouts so close together that almost no carbon dioxide and no oily froth had time to accumulate between them. In this way her lungs were cleared more completely than they ever could be with one spout. And then the young one would see that she dived vertically, so straight down that the flukes of her tail flipped out of the water as she submerged. He would sense the direction in which she dived, and with a greater thrust too; when he was near he would feel the push of the water. His mother would have done something different and therefore interesting.

He could observe a new way of diving and learn that she would be down, then, longer than usual but that did not alarm him. He played around on the surface until she would appear again, not beside him but breaking out of the water so far away that he could not see her distinctly, though he heard that she lay there, up in the air for a while, panting, before she swam back to him.

When she had sounded enough times that the long absences were becoming familiar, he felt inclined one morning to try expelling everything from his own lungs with a series of fast blows close together. On that occasion she was beside him, spouting in the same way, and then when she flung up her tail for a vertical dive, he did too and found himself head-down with all the light going quickly out of the water; but his mother was right there with her fiery streamers and her great reassuring presence.

He had not gone very far down, actually, before his

46

mother, turning so that her back was against his belly, swung him into an oblique upward course. A strangely gradual rise—the Whale might have gone back to the top as fast as he could . . . but perhaps not after all, for it was in his own instinct to return from a vertical dive on a slant. In that way the oily froth now again entering his lungs had a chance to take up the nitrogen in his blood, formed in the water's depths, before it became bubbles and endangered his life. Having oil in his lungs the Whale could cope with the gas better than human divers could, but to be safe he should allow time for the absorption of gas to take place. The slow rise had been tedious and had postponed the taking in of new oxygen, which would be welcome. But at last here they were out of the water, and the young Whale, like his mother beside him, felt inclined to lie at the surface for a few minutes, breathing deeply.

At his age he should not be allowed to go down to the maximum that a blue-whale adult might dive, which would be about half a mile. That far below the surface a whale would need the full means of adapting to the water's tremendous pressure. The food the young Whale would seek when he stopped nursing was usually not more than 600 feet down, but even at 600 feet the pressure would be 270 pounds on every square inch of his body, contrasting with 15 pounds at the surface. At half a mile there would be a pressure of 1200 pounds per square inch. There it would be necessary for the Whale's ribs to push farther and farther inward until, it might be, his lungs would actually collapse, but without damage. The lungs themselves would yield because they would have been thoroughly emptied before the dive; and the ribs would give because they were not attached to a breastbone, as most mammals' ribs are; in the front they were "floating" ribs. He would not have gasped in oxygen for the dive because he would already have an abundance of it for a dive of about 20 minutes—an excessive number of oxygen-laden red corpuscles in his blood and besides, oxygen stored in his muscles which were even reddish in color with it. Automatically the Whale would draw on those supplies when submerged; automatically too the flow of his blood would change so that most of the blood would circulate in his heart and brain while the rest of his body would suspend its demands and go into something like hibernation during the dive. Up in his head, heavy muscles would protect his eyes from the water's pressure and very dense foam would hold it away from his delicate inner ears.

Even as he went down a short way in his play or restlessness—perhaps no more than 100 feet—all these adaptations were functioning, these and others were being protection against changing pressures as he dived or came back to the surface.

During the present days of play and diving experiments the Whale and his mother had continued to migrate toward the Antarctic. They would soon go beyond the Angola Basin, passing over its southern rim into a sea where there were enough submerged highlands that the mother would stay in the water's safe upper levels. And the Whale, still guiding his actions by hers, would try no more depth dives for a while; but before the pair came away from the Basin they would go far below once again, this time the deepest yet, perhaps to a thousand feet.

On an afternoon of bright sun, when the youngster

had emptied his lungs very thoroughly and his mother hers, they turned straight down together.

The water, which was warm, 60 degrees F. at the surface, dropped to 53 degrees at 600 feet. No matter; they wouldn't be there very long. Their tails were giving their strongest strokes and soon the whales had reached the 700-foot level, 25 times the son's length, then 800 feet, then 900. It was nearly time to reverse their dive and start the gradual upward rise.

But what terrifying pulse in the water is this! The mother knew. On a wide line approaching above was a beat with a deadly regularity. It was the pace of creatures who hunt. The Whale himself had not heard that particular sound before, but his heart gave a great thump of fear. For he had an innate dread of that forward sweeping, the typical driving advance of a band of killer whales at the surface.

His mother could visualize how they were coming: a dozen or more of them stretched out horizontally, the same distance apart, the great black fins on their backs all rising together, submerging, rising with a precision, determination, in which there would never be any impulse to play. They had a motion frightfully like the propellers of whale-catching boats at South Georgia.

The mother had seen and heard killer whales there many times. They went to the feeding grounds for the same reason the killer men did: because a predictable gathering of the immense baleen whales would have been drawn to the island by the concentration of plankton. From December through April the killer men and the killer whales were certain to find a throng of victims there, although now, at the height of the antarctic winter, the island would be deserted. The men would be loafing and the killer whales would be seeking and slaughtering their prey—mammals the same as themselves—throughout other oceans.

The two kinds of killers were rivals down at South Georgia. After one of the boats had sent its fatal explosive harpoon into a mammoth whale, there would be a delay before its dead body was towed to the factory ship and drawn up inside to be "processed." During that time a band of killer whales might have an easy feast. They would snatch greedy bites out of the lips of the carcass, eat its tongue away, then the flesh of its head, its blowholes, the parts with the finest oil, most valued by men, and so the men hated the killer whales, whom they called robbers, and as well as slaughtering baleen whales they tried also to kill the killers.

The killer whales were not only after the carcasses. If none were available they pursued living whales and, being very fast swimmers, could overtake many of them. The killers' best speed was about 14 miles an hour. A fin whale could swim faster and a full-grown blue whale could also escape, but not one who was only a little more than a month old; nor could a humpback or one of the smaller species of baleen whales. And so relentless were killers that, swimming alongside one of the slower giants they would tear out its mouth even while it was fleeing. Therefore the great ones often gave up at the start of a hopeless chase. The mother of the young Whale had seen a humpback female stop trying to get away and, rolling over onto her back, had simply waited for death as a band of killer whales ate her face and tongue. From her stillness after the first terrible moments, it seemed that she died of the pain and agony, as her wounds would not have been fatal at once.

These memories undoubtedly were revived in the whale mother's mind as she heard the recognizable menace draw near. The direction from which the sound of the killers was coming was south. Therefore she and her son would start their rise also southward, hoping the killers would pass overhead and be farther north before the two had to surface.

She slid under her son so he would ride on her back. For she would determine the speed and slant of their going up, which she would make as slow as the infant could possibly stand the lack of breath and the water's pressure. The Whale himself sensed an emergency but only vaguely grasped what his mother would be attempting. As yet he was not too uncomfortable. They had not been submerged for more than five or six minutes. Ordinarily an oblique rise would get them to the top in ten minutes more, which was about the limit that he could wait at his age. But his mother was not starting up! Why was she taking so long to tilt into a slant? Why were they going along at this great depth on a level course? Instinct told him that this was not right.

The steady and fearful beat of the killer whales' swimming had grown louder and louder. Would they have heard the blue whales below? Would they dive down and attack? The possibilities were not clear in the infant's mind. He only knew that there was an ominous strangeness in the way his mother was acting.

The bright fish, bathed in glowing light, were swimming around the two whales with an indolent grace. A squid shot by. His mother should rise through the water fast, like the squid! Instead, though he could feel from her muscles that she was pushing with all her strength, there didn't seem to be any lessening of the water's pressure. They couldn't go on like this!

The sound of the killers' swimming continued its murderous hunting momentum. As they rhythmically dipped up and down through the surface, their splash filled the sea with a clamor. How different they were from the frolicking humpback whales! Or the sport of the dolphins! Or indeed of the play of the Whale himself. The killers' deliberate movement seemed fateful. Nothing could stop their coming. Unless they broke ranks, scattered their terrible purpose, this onward drive surely would end in attack.

The sound was the loudest now. But the Whale's fear was becoming dulled in the agony of his need to breathe. His lungs were full of oil and carbon dioxide and nitrogen and these were pushing against the sea's heavy pressure. He could wait no longer. He must leave his mother and dash to the top. As he started to lift away however, she rose beneath him so firmly that her motion was a command: *Stay!* But he was desperate. He must get up out of these depths. Squirming, he lifted away and she tried to relieve his distress by swimming faster.

It was a frantic ride. But the killers had gone beyond them. Slowly, oh, very slowly, the Whale and his mother were rising now. They were coming nearer the surface. But hurry! As the water's pressure grew lighter, the Whale's lungs felt as if they would burst. Then he and his mother were out, and with a great blow the Whale stretched along the top, prepared to lie there and pant as they had always done after their other deep dives. Yet this time his mother insisted that he must come down again, for even now the sounds of the killer whales were too near. They were receding but she knew how suddenly killers could swing around and come back.

Had they seen the two spouts? Apparently not, since there was no change in the frightful rhythm. She took her son underwater again, not far, keeping him out of the killers' sight until the retreating sounds diminished to almost nothing. And then they were gone, quite out of hearing, in the direction the playful dolphins had taken another day.

At last the two could relax on the surface. Gently the Whale's mother stroked her son with her flipper. He was a very dear Whale and the ending so easily could have been different.

4

The Lonely Sea

Anyone wanting to know the events of our planet's history will look first at maps. For all the past is recorded there—mountains, hills, valleys, lakes: these are the effects of happenings, some taking place slowly over a long time, and some instantaneously as when a sudden break in the earth's crust lets the molten center surge up through in a visible mass. It's a dramatic story, but less than a third of it can be read on the maps readily available. For they don't show that some of the most stupendous scenery, therefore evidence of the most stupendous events, is under the oceans—mountains miles high rising

54

out of sinks several miles deep, all unsuspected by most passengers sailing or flying over the seas. But the whales know. They live among those submerged canyons and summits. Except for shorelines, those are "the land" to whales.

One of the most spectacular is the Mid-Atlantic Ridge, 10,000 miles long and twice as wide as the Andes. It starts up beyond Iceland, swings west in an S curve between Europe and North America and, following through in another curve, becomes a lofty unbroken mountain range halfway between South America and Africa. It can be called awesomely beautiful even though no man has seen it except on the charts compiled by ships plotting the seabed with echo-locating sonar. But to the whales it is a wall—not however coming so near the surface, except here and there, that they can't swim over it. Those few places are islands which were, and even are, volcanoes erupting along the length of the Ridge and lifting its summits above the waves. Coming south from Iceland the islands are the Azores, the Saint Peter and Saint Paul Rocks (mariners are acutely aware of those), Ascension Island, Saint Helena a little off at the side, the Tristran da Cunha group, Gough Island and at the antarctic end, Bouvet. Bouvet Island, so far away and so lonely, had long been familiar to the blue whales of the South Atlantic. It is important as a rendezvous for them on their journey to the South Georgia feeding grounds.

The Whale and his mother were swimming toward Bouvet on a route between the Mid-Atlantic Ridge and Africa. They did not need to see the slopes of the Ridge in order to realize that it was there. It was known by the lesser buoyancy over its heights, by the westward current

55

that beat upon it with an upward sweep, lifting colder water to the surface, and by a change in the water's taste. The Ridge was like a vast, monumental presence, seldom seen, always sensed, and a few times brought to the whales' attention very positively.

From that wall one day came a living voice, a great pulsing, thrumping voice obviously from a creature with massive strength. And whereas the humpback's song had sounded as if it were raised for the singer's own satisfaction, the mountain voice was more clearly a call. Or at least an announcement: *I am here, a great blue whale, a male who is solitary and lonely.* Even to human ears, when that voice was recorded, it seemed to be an appeal. To the Whale's mother, who recognized it as a whale of her own species, it apparently had additional meaning. As if stirred by it, she made a few quick tail splashes and speeded her swimming pace. She didn't turn toward the voice, nor answer it, because active courtships would not be an interest in blue whales now in August. Except in the spring the sexual urges of any blue male are quiescent; and the female would not be tempted until after her young one was weaned. But loneliness knows no season, and for these whales, who form lasting pair bonds, that kind of companionship could be a real need at any time. And so the mother, alone, as the male sounded, seemed to find the voice of the male sympathetically moving.

He continued to call. It was a three-syllable message and curiously with the intervals established in human music. A long tone on the fifth, or dominant note dropped to the next lower keynote *(sol* to *do),* held briefly there and then dropped a further half note, the falling away seeming the most sad, although it was lightened by an overtone an octave above. The call had the same sequence each time, and it filled the ocean for a vast distance—more than 700 miles in all directions. Human listeners measuring its volume as recorded with hydrophones have said that the blue-whale call is as loud as one of the great United States Navy cruisers proceeding at normal speed. They describe the call as having a strength of 180 decibels. The sound waves, coming through water, were felt all over the whales' sensitive skin and of course in their ears as well. They were so low that they were like throbs; in fact the pitch of the three tones were only distinguished for human listeners by increasing the speed of the sound waves mechanically. But even without knowing technically what a full, rich, musical call it was, a human being could feel an emotional longing in it.

The mountain voice would be heard by the whales again. But this time it was drowned out by a greater roaring. The new sound began as a very strange rumble, faint but quickly growing in volume. It wasn't a living voice; it was made up of thousands of smaller knocks, objects apparently striking each other or falling on others below them. The whole soon became deafening and seemed threatening, indeed terrifying, and the whales went up to swim along close to the surface.

The disturbance became a tumult. To the waves of sound at the beginning now were added literal waves breaking the top of the water. The whales went ahead faster, and the young one sensed that his mother was panicky and confused. For what was happening to their world?

The lonely male had amazingly started this. Just as

a pistol shot can set off an avalanche of snow in the visible mountains on continents, a landslide can be caused under the sea by a sound sufficiently loud. At the call of the male an outthrust spur on the side of the Ridge had crumbled away from the slope behind it and was crashing down onto the seabed below. A descending mass of rocks and old lava, it was going down ponderously because of the water's resistance.

As more and more rocks were added to the debris the heavy rumbling became louder still, and a wide turbulence reached the surface. It was bringing up mud and the unseen, countless bodies of tiny plankton animals crushed by the impact or suffocated by clouds of silt. Only after a very long time and with a few delayed repercussions did the din cease; and even more gradually the water quieted. It had been one of the earth's events that might require maps to be changed, although this caving away of a mountainside might not be known for years by the cartographers, if it ever would be.

The whales' route took them next through one of the pleasantest seas on earth: the lower Atlantic Ocean in the horse latitudes. The skies were fair and the water so glossy-still that once when the Whale lifted his head and shoulders to look around, he could see his reflection in it. During the several days that he and his mother spent on this placid pond in the sea, there seemed to be no wind at all. Yet the water was not stagnant because a fringe-flow from the Benguela Current crossed it, slowly, not strong enough to carry a ship along very fast. The easy weather had not pleased the crews of early sailing ships who were becalmed here while trying to take cargoes of horses to South America. The horses that did make a landfall gave a start to that breed of splendid riders, the Gauchos, but too often the ships and their living cargoes were immobilized for so long that food for the horses ran out and the starving animals were thrown overboard.

The young Whale was not hungry. Since he was born, ten weeks earlier, he had grown to be 35 feet long and had increased his weight from two tons to twenty. Those extra tons had been transferred to him with his mother's milk; they were subtracted from her own normal weight and she was beginning to feel that she would welcome the chance to eat again. But there was no point in hurrying. If they arrived at South Georgia before the first of November ice would still cover the krill in the ocean. Mid-November would be about the right time; and meanwhile there might be a chance now and then en route to assuage the worst pangs of hunger. When they did reach the great feeding grounds they could easily catch all the krill their stomachs could hold—more than two tons a day by the mother, less for the Whale until he had grown proficient in feeding himself. It would be the antarctic summer there, not summer as it was known in the Whale's home place or even in the horse latitudes. It would be a summer studded with ice. Meanwhile, idling along at 20 to 25 miles a day, the two gave themselves to the sunny spirit of the mild sea here.

Animal young, even more than human children, by instinct promote their own physical development—they teach themselves what they need to learn. Any blue whale would eventually have to take his vast bulk through the water fast and flexibly, which would require ever stronger muscles and the subtle use of them; therefore the young one had an impulse to play in the ways that would build those muscles and show him the possibilities in his element.

He liked to dive straight down, make a quick upward flip and at the top straighten out to ripple along the surface. He rolled under and over in one somersault after another, coming to rest belly uppermost with the sun warming the grooves on his throat—those accordion pleats that would allow his mouth to expand into a great cavity later, when he would be taking in swarms of krill. He splashed with his tail and flippers, perhaps challenging an imaginary playmate. Then, spiraling down and spiraling up again, he would hang motionless in the water until, with a surge of his tail, he would streak away, impossible to catch if any enemy should have such an idea, meanwhile making glittering bow waves along his sides. And often he just moved about rather slowly, swinging as far sidewise as a rather unyielding neck would allow, to left, to right, at play with the water as if it were a sexual partner, feeling its stroking along his skin, its resistance, its giving way, and in all this as graceful as swallows, making his first moves toward learning what could be a real sexual water-dance some day. To that, which would call for the most limber and skillful motion, all his present play would contribute, even though he had no intimation now of that future advantage.

But always of course he must breathe—always that, whether playing, feeding, chasing companions or fleeing in fright there would be this relentless need to come up

to the surface. And that was part of his practice: to inter-
rupt whatever he did and return to the top to blow.

The Whale's play with his mother here also would
help, although she found his swimming too youthful, too
fast, indeed too joyful to enter into it as a wholly inspir-
ing partner. Her own swimming often appeared to be
done for pleasure, but of a milder kind, and when she
swam with her son she was more a pivot for his bold
tumbles than a tumbler herself. Nevertheless he often
would try to tempt her into a game even if it was only
a form of swimming together, side by side, with his mother's great body creating whirlpools down there in the
glossy depths.

Then when he was tired, he lay on her body, either
her back or belly, or beside her with one of her flippers
under him and their sides touching all the way down to
his tail. She stroked him, and sometimes he just explored
different ways to feel the glide of his skin over hers. For
these whales have a very sensitive skin and one of their
satisfactions is the tactile smoothing of one's skin against
that of another. In their twilight world and with eyes that
have imperfect vision, they lack the diversion that land
animals have in just looking and watching: but touch is
a more immediate way to experience outwardness and
they spend much time in the skin-feeling of another whale's
presence. Among human beings the sensations of touch
are most often associated with sexuality. Blue whales,
however, are not lascivious creatures. Very intense in
their lovemaking, they are limited in such urges to May,
June and July, but they don't therefore abandon tactile
communication the rest of the year. With an affectionate
mother that was something else the young Whale was

learning: the simple companionship that is expressed by touch.

And with the ocean so quiet, the Whale also discovered that he could nurse underwater. That skill would be useful when they were among the killer-men's boats and were trying to stay out of sight. There the sea would be tossed into violent waves on most days; but now, having learned how to grasp his mother's nipple while holding his breath, he would be able to do that in any weather. Although he would be starting to get his own food, the krill, at South Georgia, he would still have to be able to nurse from time to time.·

For the present here in the horse latitudes the days passed with sunshine gliding across the polished sea, with no clouds in the sky and no further landslides. The light breezes were ruffling the water so gently that webs of light played on the mother's back. The young Whale tried to touch them but then the shining reflections were transferred to his own nose and flippers where he only caught glimpses of them. The wavelets were teasing him. He splashed at the surface and the reflections, too, splashed.

The mountain male called now and then and the Whale's mother answered, in a way, by lobtailing—a slight message, only a small sign that she might be interested later. Wherever he was, his route seemed to parallel that of herself and her son, which was not strange at this time of year when most blue whales headed south.

These days might have been a whale's idyll except that the two had acquired some unwelcome and worrisome riders. There were three kinds, the most annoying being some amphipods, like two-inch crabs with claws ending in hooks which fastened into the whales' tender skin and held them there while the so-called "whale lice" *(Cyamus)* ate a pit into which they cozily settled, eating more and more deeply. They would die and drop off when the whales came to seas strewn with ice, but scars would remain, gray freckles on the whales' dark skin that they would carry for the rest of their lives.

Smaller parasites *(Pennela)* had dug in and anchored themselves with prongs that spread apart, horribly like the great prongs on the men's explosive harpoons. Those would leave no scars when they too died of the cold and the whales' skin would repair the wounds. Nor would the most conspicuous of the parasites: *Conchoderma* barnacles, growing on stalks and looking very like crocuses. They took their food from the surrounding water, from plankton, only using the skin of the whales as other barnacles use the hulls of ships: as vehicles to carry them through the nourishing seas. They too would be gone in a few months, but in the meantime, having fastened themselves mostly around their hosts' heads, they gave the whales a jaunty look, as if they wore wreaths of blossoms.

All this time the whales had been progressing southward and rather suddenly found themselves in a very different kind of weather and seas that were mountain-high. These were the Roaring Forties, the 40's south latitude, dreaded by sailors but the Whale responded with gusto. Now he was learning something that he would know even better before long: what the sea's wildest fury was like. It was a challenge! He dove under the biggest waves, sometimes waiting until they started to break, which seemed dangerous and exciting. And then he learned a wonderful game: swinging lengthwise to lie in the crest of a wave as it was mounting up to its greatest height, he found it would carry him forward at breathless speed. Just before the wave broke he would duck down and then catch a ride in another one, oncoming from the west. His mother had learned to do the same thing long ago but she was not in a mood for that kind of fun at her age and in this place and time. She was staying below, where the immense movement was only a roll. The pair were, as a matter of fact, in the West Wind Drift, which —drift—sounds mild but it was a band in the sea where steadily blowing gales from Cape Horn kept the water in a cold tumult.

To the mother this sea was almost as familiar as the nearby small Tristan da Cunha islands were to the mollymauks, petrels, and shearwaters that nested on them. The fast flow from westward, the wind-driven heaving, and most important, the flavor of krill were always remembered. The water tasted of krill because it had passed over the South Georgia feeding grounds where small numbers of krill had been snatched up to be carried along on this current. To fasting whales on their way south to the great feast, or on their return to their summer sea, this chance to enjoy a few stomachfuls of their favorite food kept them here in this region for several days. Now with the youngster the mother might stay again except that this time she had something else on her mind.

Five months ago on their way back she and her mate had stopped in these waters, trying to find a few last euphausids. That time they were scarce, however, and the two whales, in their eager hunting, had become widely separated. They were keeping in touch with their voices although some calls were lost in the roar and crash of the hurtling waves. Gradually then the pregnant female (the little Whale would be born in six weeks) became conscious that she had not heard her mate for some time.

There had been sounds of a boat not far away, and those too had been lost and found and lost again in the confusion of noisy waters. And another sound . . . had it really been a sound? Or was it only the memory that haunted any whale who had been at the feeding grounds? It was the most sickening sound on earth per-haps—the sound of exploding flesh. For four months she had heard it all day, every day. But she could expect that it would fade slowly; it always had, drowned by the affectionate voice of her mate and later by the whimpers of a small whale. But it was more persistent this time— a thud not long ago? Fairly near?

Suddenly in a panic she began swimming back and forth, constantly calling, calling. There was never an an-swer. Not even the sound of the boat—but yes. A boat's engines, after having been silent, had started up again. Made bold by anxiety she sped directly toward the sound, surfaced—and saw her mate being towed away, belly uppermost. One of his severed flukes floated near. If there had been any sign that he was alive, however feebly, she would have gone to him without hesitation. She would have gone into certain death to be near him. But most animals recognize death, and know it is final, and she turned away.

Day after sorrowing day, then, she had proceeded alone to the summer sea where she bore this infant.

None of her other four offspring had been so welcome as this one, especially needed to ease her loneliness. Now they were back in the same waters where she had lost the Whale's father, and so far on their migration the only sign that there were other blue whales in the sea had been the voice of the mountain male.

When she had been only a year or two old, blue whales had been scarce. There was even a doubt whether she ever would find a mate. But one year at South Georgia, when there were almost as many whale-catching boats as whales, a very strange ship had sailed into that ocean. It seemed like a whale itself, long and slim, and amazingly it stayed under the surface and didn't kill whales. With weapons that looked like whale-killing harpoons, it struck the whale-catching boats, which sank with their crews—all but a few that steamed away very fast. And then for five years or more there were no killer men at the feeding grounds. Blue whales were supreme in the sea, as they had been for the millions of years before killer men ever came. Their population was not as large as it once had been, but it was increasing—that was the great thing. There was again a prospect of ongoing life for blue whales: the earth's largest and gentlest, harmless and intelligent creatures were not going to vanish. That new expectation after despair could be sensed in the very way they moved, fearless and strong when they came together en route to South Georgia. The Whale's mother had been one of the first of the young to find a mate but so did others, and new infants began to appear with their migrating parents. The recent hopelessness was dispelled, almost forgotten. And when the migrants reached the annual feeding grounds and found there hundreds, thousands of other blue whales, they assumed that the human killers were gone, now, for good—this was the whales' world once more, and the sea boiled with frisky titans, able to play, to feed, to relax without caution. It seemed as if all the whales here had become young again.

That had been a false spring, however. After the respite new killer men came to replace the ones who had been torpedoed; and blue whales died in such numbers at South Georgia that this route to the feeding grounds was almost deserted. On the last trip the Whale's parents had made, they had seen only one other blue, a young female, either coming or going.

If the Whale had not already been growing inside his mother, he might never have been conceived. For it seemed that a robust kind of joy was required if a pair of good companions felt their love bursting out in physical exaltation. Mates could take comfort in each other's presence, they could be drawn together by their very sadness when their species seemed to be dying out; but that kind of tenderness did not boil up into sexual play. As with all animals that were nearing extinction, blue whales everywhere were bearing fewer and fewer young. They were mating in the sense of choosing loving companions, but the companionship was a shared sorrow.

Now the Whale's mother didn't even have that, but what would happen when the two of them reached Bouvet Island? Perhaps this year there would be more blue whales coming together there. It would not take an immense amount of encouragement to make the adults feel that blue whales had a future after all. And what of the young Whale himself? When the time came for him to mate, after a few more years, would he want a female to share discouragement, or one to join him in a celebration of high spirits? He had made a fine start if his growth into maturity was to be a journey toward joy.

5

Summer and Ice

The men who killed the Whale's father had come from a station on Africa's coast near the Cape of Good Hope. The station had been established there because the waters around the Cape were a crossroads for whales—all kinds of whales going east and west and at other times north and south. Formerly they had passed in tremendous numbers; now there were fewer but still enough for the station to operate during the spring and autumn when whales were known to be migrating.

It was tempting for whales to stop near the Cape for a few days because there was a curious basin of very

70

warm water just south of the continent. The Agulhas Current, which had flowed down the east coast of Africa from the hot Indian Ocean, rounded the Cape but there met the stronger, cold West Wind Drift and was turned east again. This tropical pool in the sea inspired the young one to play again and his mother to be indulgent. He was the liveliest of the infants that she had borne, and she had come to share, somewhat, his eager interest in everything, his delight in being alive. Could she also have been aware that the longer their migration lasted, the longer he would stay with her, this most lovable of her offspring and the only companion, now, that she had? She was increasingly hungry, a sensation that must have reminded her that she had no choice but to continue the rest of the way to the waters around South Georgia, fertile with her kind of food but fertile also with explosive harpoons. Needing to go, wishing to stay, she idled here, only now and then expressing her dread of the dangers ahead with a rumbling sigh.

The Whale wandered away from her, farther than usual but he was not frightened; he had only to send back an echo signal and know exactly where he could return to her. Meanwhile he had made an exciting discovery. By bending down very steeply he could catch a glimpse of the undersides of his fan-shaped flukes, their splash into view and quick disappearance timed with his motion of arching them. As he tried this again and again he sent some clicks from his head to his tail and the echoes returned: a talk with himself! . . . but a game suddenly interrupted by a tremendous clamor as six strange new whales bolted up from the seabed and surfaced.

They were sperm whales, a group of bachelors

roaming the seas between their mating seasons in the Pacific Ocean. Although they were unfamiliar the young one had no instinctive fear of them; no inherited dread suggested that these—twice as large as killer whales— would attack as the killers would. They seemed very boistrous and in several ways grotesque. Most creatures the young one had seen were streamlined, other whales and fish: surely nature's preferred shape for marine animals. But these looked like great tubes of flesh, thickest up at their heads, so that the sperms had to plough along behind a huge boxlike snout, off-center, for their right nostrils were enlarged into "tanks," as men called them, which held a ton of spermaceti wax, valuable as a lubricant; and the rest of the head would yield 30 barrels of oil. The sperms were breathing through their left nostrils only, so placed that their spouts came out of the side of their heads and pointed obliquely forward. And all these remarkable whales were decorated with circular scars six inches across, because the sperms fed on the giant squids of the ocean floor, and while the whales were trying to swallow the squids the victims clung with suction cups to the skin around the whales' heads and only let go when they pulled away discs of flesh.

The scars proved that the squids did fight. Inconceivable, monstrous struggles must have taken place in the black depths of the abyssal seabed: a writhing, clutching combat between the whale, 60 feet long, with its teeth in the body of the squid, and the squid whose immense arms wound sinuously around the whale's head, attaching its dozens of suction cups. Yet it seemed obvious that the sperm whales must relish this kind of entanglement, for, as the Whale watched, a six-foot squid jetted by and most of the sperms ignored such a puny adversary. But one of them opened his mouth, took it in and swallowed it, and the Blue Whale had a chance to see that the sperm's mouth too was bizarre, for it was not at the front of the head but underneath and with teeth, very long and sharp, on only the lower jaw while the upper jaw had sockets into which the teeth fitted. This arrangement suggested a halfway evolution from teeth to baleen. Because they had no baleen, no means of straining out plankton food, there would not be many sperms at the South Georgia feeding grounds. But the ones who did wander through would be killed—for their oil and for the chance of finding that strange substance, ambergris, which occasionally accumulated in their intestines and was highly valued as a fixative for perfume. The ambergris also imparted a delicate floral fragrance of its own—curiously, for the meat and oil of the sperms had an odor that was considered repulsive by most men, and by the Whale, when he took in a breath just after the sperms had exhaled and he found it a stench.

The travelers were entertaining however. As they disported themselves between the Whale and his mother, they threw themselves about, raising steep-sided waves—and now one of them did something altogether astonishing. He made a fairly deep dive, quickly reversed and with a tremendous thrust of his tail, shot himself upright out of the surface, so far that he stood vertically, all but his flukes in the air, for an instant. And was this position in some prophetic way a congenial performance to the young Blue? Did it stir an inherited impulse in him? Did it make the sperm whales, so outrageous otherwise, seem almost like kin? And had his mother, too, been moved to action? For now she dived under the sperm whales to come up at the side of her son, and at first she seemed strangely excited.

At the sight of her the Whale suddenly realized that he was hungry, and so the two of them quieted down while he nursed. . . and afterward left, continuing south toward Bouvet Island and colder water.

Later that day the Whale and his mother also met several fin whales, more like themselves in size, shape and ways of moving but still not their own kind. These were going east, bound for the coast of Australia where they would find krill but not in such quantities as would be at South Georgia. Many fin whales apparently were inclined to swim toward the rising sun, whereas blue whales had an internal compass that usually sent them westward. That was only one thing that made fin whales seem different. Although slim and graceful they had peculiar color markings, white on dark gray and different on the right and left sides. Even the black insides of their mouths had white patches not alike on left and right; alien whales they were, friendly enough but their presence did nothing to relieve the desolation of the mother. As they were leaving she called a few times, not to them, only as though reminded that they were not blues. It was a muted sound, hardly more than a sigh. There was not much chance of its reaching anyone and that probably was not her intention. It seemed only the voice of loneliness.

After another day she came out of her sad absorption and they left the warm current here—so abruptly that one moment they were in waters of 72 degrees F., and by swimming little more than their own length they found the sea to be 60 degrees and the next day 42 degrees. It would become colder. And with the crisper temperature, wonderfully their luck turned and here did come three other blue whales, like themselves and obviously migrating in the accepted direction. They apparently had spent the warm months off the opposite coast of Africa and now were making the journey around the Cape, they too bound across the Atlantic Ocean for South Georgia. They were a family of parents and a young nursing female and joining the other two, they started along the route to Bouvet Island.

For these five the swimming ahead was a harmony wonderful to experience. It was a braiding, weaving movement, swinging apart and together again, cruising along with their species rhythm, all in the same direction, at the same pace, to the same goal, in the congeniality of all being the largest animals ever, all being gentle, all with the same sort of grace. With no other species could the five have known the mutual feeling they had with these easy companions. And so the time passed very pleasantly as they proceeded, the parents of the young female, like the Blue-Whale's mother, holding back their speed slightly to the ability of their immature offspring.

They were the first of his own species the young Whale had seen, and he was inspired to put on a show of extra fine swimming. Once he came up to surface beside the juvenile female, slapping her with his flipper, but the effect was disappointing: she was startled and swam away to her mother. The Whale's own mother had become livelier, with more talk, as though her spirits had brightened at the proof that there were other blue whales in the sea.

Not far ahead a mountain peak would become visible—Bouvet, which was a small island known to men as the loneliest place on earth, there being no other land in any direction for more than a thousand miles. But blue whales always approached it with the anticipation that there they would find other whales of their kind, and it was with that hope that the little company pressed on to the rendezvous.

When they had been traveling together for only two days, the five whales were further cheered by another's arrival. They heard him before they saw him—at first only a pulse in the water, the strokes of his powerful swimming. Next, besides the evidence on their skins, came a voice, one recognized by the Whale and his mother. It was the same call they had heard from the mountains, a blue's typical three tones but with something more: a poignant urgency—and amazingly musical, a pitch too low for human ears to identify, yet known to be in the scale that so many birds and singing mammals seem to be reaching for, though usually with less success than the blue whale's. His could have been the theme for a song.

The five had been chattering in lighter tones and the distant male may have heard them for he was certainly coming to find them. A splendid male he was when he appeared, plunging ahead, pushing the ocean away on each side of him in a bow wave. He was slightly smaller than the Whale's mother, for most male blues did not quite attain the length of the females; but he was a male in his prime, moving with fine precision and forcefulness. After he joined the others there was a diving and splashing that lasted for several hours, a liveliness like a celebration. For these adult whales were reassured, after a time when they had known the slackening of morale that comes to most animals when they sense that their numbers have drastically declined. They would be going along contentdly now, made resilient by the companionship of their kind, deeply confident that the conditions for their continued existence were favorable.

The young Whale was finding the colder water here stimulating, but within a few days the sea became curiously different. Now the water was thicker, heavier. There was a gale one day yet the water didn't respond to it much. A wave would not lift to a great crest that flung off its spray and then tumbled over in inviting foam that made a whale want to dive into it. The water did rise in large swells but ponderously, something to labor through rather than play with. What the Whale didn't understand was that here the water was full of ice crystals, too small to see, too small even to feel with sensitive skin except as a still colder temperature. It was water that was beginning to freeze.

Ice was something he soon would know better. One morning there was an iceblink on the horizon—the shine of an ice field reflected up on low-hanging clouds. And then, on a bright day, the travelers came among sparkling white knobs and pans of ice, almost like foam but glittering. The Whale rose more often into the air for the sheer enjoyment of being dazzled. He slapped a small ice pan and broke it into a splash of brilliant white bits, like sun-dust. He dropped his chin onto another pan and sparklets sprayed all around him. Seeing what fun he was having, the young female too began slapping ice, drenching herself with light.

The adults were finding patches of their own food and from time to time they paused in their migration to eat. The two young ones, still not having baleen to strain out the krill, were nursing and between times were playing about in this unfamiliar world. They swam along streams of clear water between the ice pans, or wandered together beneath the ice, which made a pearly twilight below, strange and mysterious.

And then, as the adults worked their way farther south, and the young with them, they came upon icebergs, some of them flat-topped and large, others of fantastic shapes where they had been broken up during gales. Between them most of the surface was covered with clumps of ice which had been sheared off the bergs. These, "the growlers," kept up a grumbling combined with tinkling sounds as the sea's movement crushed them together. They did not progress over the surface, but among them the icebergs, catching the wind and pushed ahead by it, were all moving along majestically.

The young Whale investigated one of the icebergs. It didn't look so immense when seen from above the surface, but underneath it was a great mass of ice hanging down in the water, the part below being many times larger than what was visible in the air. The Whale approached cautiously. It was not black-dark, as for example his mother's body was underwater: the berg faintly glowed with light coming through it down from above. The Whale sent out his signals against it and they returned fast and sharply. He went closer and dared to touch the ice, finding it harder than anything else he had ever encountered. He had always lived in a yielding world; the sea and all the creatures in it were pliant, or at least soft to a prodding snout. But not this iceberg. If one rammed it a whale could injure himself. Hardness—amazing.

Ahead in the distance was a high mass that, unlike the icebergs, did not move: Bouvet Island. As the adults led in that direction, the young played about, though in water increasingly dark, for a snowstorm, covering the ice field, shut out the light. Meanwhile the whales had to be careful not to get themselves under a floe so thick and wide that they couldn't rise for air when they needed to. The parents knew conditions like these and they were keeping watch on their offspring as they became acquainted with the delights and dangers of ice.

Suddenly the Whale's echo signals reported that an unfamiliar creature was swimming nearby. It certainly wasn't a whale; it was an animal with a strangely shaped head, flippers that seemed to move with almost as limber a turning as the remembered arms of the human boatman; and it had fins but no flukes. It was no fish either, and no animal like an octopus; but it was large, almost as long as the Whale was when he was born and much heavier. It had a thick, massive body and yet it moved with the most dexterous grace. Now it came up to the surface and the Whale put his head out of the water to see it more clearly.

The seal—for that's what it was, a young bull elephant seal—had an astonishing nose, at first seeming a normal snout, though crossed with deep wrinkles, but then as he took a new breath the nose flared out, a fleshy bulb that protruded some inches beyond his face. The seal scratched the nose with the nails at the end of his foreflipper and the Whale, fascinated, watched. He himself could not have done that, since his own flippers lacked the muscles to bend them and had no nails.

The seal submerged and turned toward the island and the Whale followed. With this closer view he could see that the island was almost solidly ringed with icebergs, large ones resting upon the seabed, but there was an opening through this barrier, between two of the bergs. The seal took that way to go into the water beyond, which was like a small lake with a few broken pans of ice but no solid cover. The Whale went in too.

On the beach was a sight like nothing under the sea. Many more bulls, huge old males, were surrounding harems of docile cows, and off at the edge were younger bulls with no cows of their own. One of the bachelors splashed in the shallows and it roared a challenge when the bull from the ocean approached. The two started to fight, raising themselves chest to chest, to draw back and butt each other in head and neck. They bashed with their foreflippers and thrust their long snouts into each other's faces, a deadly combat it seemed but was probably only a practice fight, for they bared their long teeth but neither slashed into the other's hide.

The Whale's mother had come to get him away from this shore and back with their other companions, who had found a good patch of krill and were gulping down mouthfuls. She had been calling her son but in his excitement he had not heard her. Even now he did not sense that her voice was urgent. There was not only the sparring of the two bachelor seals in the shallows to watch, but a few late matings were going on, the great bulls going from cow to cow in the harems, while above on the shingle the bachelors restlessly prowled or looked on, with their heads and hindflippers lifted until they touched, making the shape of the seal a hoop. The Whale never, it seemed, would tire of observing such fantastic creatures.

Then the young bull from the sea made a discovery over his challenger's shoulder. One of the cows was straying away from the beachmaster. Perhaps she could be seduced! The mock battle abandoned, the young bull hoisted himself on shore and with a heavy and clumsy motion, utterly unlike his grace in the water, was crossing the beach. He would hump his hind end under him and then pull ahead with his foreflippers—hump and drag, hump and drag, looking especially awkward because he was trying to hurry.

The old bull who was ruler of the cow's harem had seen what was happening. Humping himself along to the cow, only half his size, he took her neck in his teeth and threw her back with his other cows and then turned to face the rival.

In some such fight the young bull would defeat the old one and acquire all his cows at a stroke. Perhaps this was the time! Both bellowing, the two crashed together. They reared, each thrusting with all his weight, pounding against the other's head and slashing across head and chest with sharp, gleaming teeth. Blood flowed copiously from both necks; both the great mouths were wide as they thundered their anger. But the fight seemed to lack tension, for the two immense mounds of blubbery flesh shook like jelly.

Slaps were falling upon the Whale himself—his

mother demanding that he should come away and at once. The Whale hardly felt the blows; he was too absorbed in the sight of raw combat between the two grotesque animals—two of the same species. Such a fight between two blue whales would be so unnatural as to be out of the question. But a fight with an animal of a different kind? Deep, never displayed, there was in the young Whale's instincts a buried rage that someday might possess him if he were ever attacked by an alien enemy. But who could that be, since he was no longer an infant and soon would be larger and stronger than all other creatures? An unlikely attack—and yet as he watched the seals, the possibility of a desperate anger may have stirred in him. For he rebelliously stayed though his mother continued to slap and was prodding him with her snout.

The bachelor seal leaped away from his combat to try to cut out a cow at the edge of a different harem. He was mounting the cow when her master caught up and flung himself on the pair. Other young bachelors attempted then to snatch cows. Skin and flesh and blood flew in all directions and the bellowing echoed from Bouvet's mountain and from the icebergs encircling the beach. The whole company was in turmoil.

The young Whale held his head out of the water, nearsighted eyes straining to follow one fracas and then another. His mother, pushing him, toppled him over. With a protest, the first time his voice had ever expressed defiance, he struggled upright. His mother turned back. If he would not obey, she would leave him. But . . . stop! What frightful thing is this? An iceberg, driven along by the wind, is sailing across the whales' only exit into the

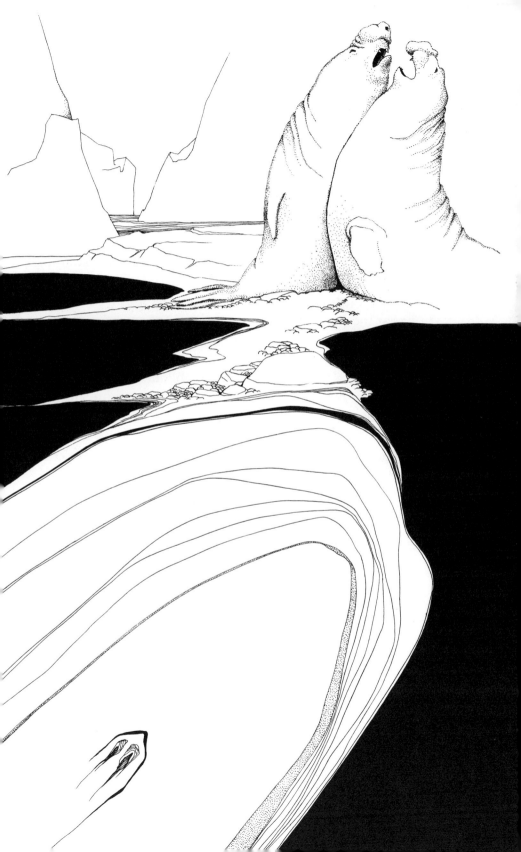

sea beyond. It will continue to pass, no doubt, leaving the way of escape as it was before. Now it has closed the slot but is still moving.

The Whale's particular seal had given up and, bleeding from many tears in his hide, had retreated. The rest of the fights, too, had been resolved; in each case the older, more experienced bull had vanquished the would-be usurper. The Whale, his excitement spent, slid back under the water and found his mother, who was awaiting the chance to break out of the wall of ice.

But tides and waves had built up a submerged sand-bar at the point in the seabed where the other, surrounding icebergs had deflected the water's flow. The new iceberg was still progressing, but slowly. Its scraping upon the sandbar was causing a sibilant crunch, perhaps ominous to the mother. With a final jolt and a shudder the iceberg came to a stop. At its stern end the berg tapered down to a shelf, two or three feet below the sea's surface. Rearing their heads, the whales could see over it, but they could not escape.

6

Escape into Danger

To the young Whale the fact of their being trapped was not in itself alarming; for as long as his mother was with him, with her immense size and her milk, the situation must be all right. When he nudged her, wanting to nurse, that first day, a few times she turned away. Strange and not good. He felt the beginnings of fright.

Their companions, the small family and single male, saw what had happened and the adults may have sensed its significance. They gathered outside the obstructing iceberg. The two who were behind the barrier could see over the shallow ice ledge but they were unable to cross it nor could their friends, although they came as close as they could. For the rest of the afternoon all of them called back and forth. The ones outside went on feeding on krill, stopping from time to time to send over assurances of their concern.

The Whale turned to watch the seals but with less interest now. There were no fights and the matings seemed all alike, casual and perfunctory—utterly different from the mating of blue whales, though he would know that only by intuition. The bull seals would cover their cows, their great bulk seeming to smother them, and immediately go on to others. The Whale swam about in this lake for a while, frustrated at coming so soon to its walls. At the day's end their companions drew farther away and his mother sank into a mood of foreboding.

In the morning the ones who were free sent again their vocal comfort to those who were trapped. Idling at the surface the mother ceaselessly watched for them over the ledge. At noon the other whales disappeared and the voices were heard no more. She called again and again but there was no answer and after a while she became silent. She seemed to accept the thought that the others had left to continue on to the feeding grounds. Their departure might mean they believed her outlook was hopeless. She herself seemed to feel that it was.

The young Whale was bored. He ignored the seals and, as well, two other kinds of creatures here at Bouvet —Cape pigeons and penguins. In other waters he would have been curious about them, especially the penguins, but his own youthful instinct told him, too, that they should be leaving this island; they should be strongly forcing their way through an ice-cluttered sea. To go, to be spending his ever-maturing strength, to be gaining speed: all this was a terribly urgent impulse, impossible to relieve. He alternated between a wild thrashing about and lethargic tonelessness.

Many stagnant days passed. Other blue whales sometimes came past the island, not lingering since their migration was late. Most were families, parents with single young. Once there would have been several such groups coming through every day. Now there were only two or three in a week, and the lonely mother inside the barrier may have sensed again the falling away of the blue-whale numbers. By the end of November no more of them traveled this route.

She had long since consumed the sparse krill inside the ice and now she was famished. It was normal for blue-whale mothers to give about half their weight to their infants. Although the 96-foot length of the Whale's mother made her a large female her weight was only average, 130 tons, when he was born. After the essential transfer of her body's nourishment to her son she would have weighed something like 65 tons and by then she should have been voraciously eating again at South Georgia. But as one month and then two went by at Bouvet Island she lost weight to 55 tons and then 46. She was pathetically thin, starving really. Yet always willingly she rolled over to let the Whale have her milk when he wanted it.

The icebergs continued to hold their position around the bay. On clear days the sun was warm enough to form meltwater which dripped off the surfaces but did not lessen the bulk of the ice beneath. No ice ever had looked more beautiful—glittering white and translucent blue—and never had seemed more deadly. The ledge on the last, imprisoning berg was still two or three feet below the top of the water, and the mass of ice under it extended all the way to the sandy bottom.

The elephant seals could get over the ledge. They were half-stranded when they were on it but then they would propel themselves along with their foreflippers. They went out every day to find food in the ocean depths, for their matings had ended and a season of indolence was at hand. After foraging for a few hours the seals would come back to the beach where they would lie and doze, constantly scratching the furry hides of their winter coats with facile "fingers" and nails, scratching even in sleep. The antarctic summer, now nearing its height, was a vacation for them, a time for all far-southern animals to enjoy themselves.

For the imprisoned pair this restraint was not being a whale. This was not whaleness. Whaleness was giving a swoop with one's tail and shooting ahead to the boundaries of the earth! Skin glistening smooth sliding through glossy yielding of water.

Whaleness was utter freedom, no gravity and no walls. A body able to curl itself in great arcs or, straightening out, glide forward with effortless ease. Men spoke enviously of being as free as a bird. They should say free as a whale, for birds were limited by the exertion needed to stay in the air whereas a whale's floating was weightless, his swimming simply a wish become motion.

But no longer. Locked in by the ice, the Whale and his mother learned what it was to live in narrow and barren confinement. Sometimes they gave a few thrusts with their flukes just to feel again what it was like to sweep along through slippery water: supremely power-ful! But they had to brake with their flippers quickly to keep from striking the hardness of ice. No longer free, no longer knowing true whaleness. Squeezed into a form of nonliving. For a whale a slow, final agony.

Death.

Next to moving in a wide welcoming sea—the splendor of it!—they missed the motion of water itself, hurtling waves to tumble about in, to smash through, to ride on, to wait below as the breakers passed overhead sensuously rolling a submerged whale from side to side, elegant secret play.

But there were no waves here. Lifeless water lying empty of movement except for some trivial ripples on top. When a seal came in over the ledge and splashed to the beach stirring up silt, the silt remained in the water that hadn't even the sway to disperse it.

This pond inside the ice borders so cramped the Whale's action that his muscles ached from constraint. Therefore he lobtailed often, raising his flukes high in the air and then crashing them down on the surface. Noise at least, but no substitute for a vigorous dashing ahead. Sometimes he took three or four swings toward the shore, as if wanting to strand himself—but checked the onward plunge in time and turned instead to a nudge at his mother so strong it was almost a ramming. She struck back with her snout and ill feeling threatened to rise between them: amazing! Impossible. That didn't happen with blue whales and she turned the anger into a sad little moment of play, followed by gentle comfort-ing . . . before they both relapsed again into lying pas-sively in the water, appearing hopeless.

The weather had remained calm almost all the time the two had been here. Then one morning the sky was heavy and dark and a new strong wind from the west was whistling around the icebergs. The mother, after being listless during the quiet days, was stimulated to swim back and forth, whipping her flukes impatiently as she turned about. It seemed that she would crash through the ice wall if she could.

That effort would have been futile but she did something just as effective. In a desperate move she hurled herself onto the ledge that extended out from one side of the iceberg that had closed off their exit. Though she had lost so much weight there were still nearly 50 tons of whale now bearing down on the ledge. With a loud snap of splitting ice the berg capsized, throwing the mother into deep water, the water outside the barrier. The young Whale was still within, but the turning up of the iceberg had released it from the sandbar below, and in the strong wind of that day the berg was driven away, gradually opening the space that had existed before the berg ever became immobilized here. The Whale immediately sped through and found his mother—out in the wide ocean with its invitation to enjoy their restored freedom.

They left for South Georgia immediately. For a while they had been exceptional, long-staying visitors here at Bouvet, and then they were gone and months would pass before any other blue whales would come by. Bouvet Island would once more be the most remote place on earth, but not of course remote to the creatures who lived there. Bouvet was the center of the universe to its seals and penguins and pigeons.

There had been one compensation for the whales' imprisonment: during those weeks the parasites in their flesh had succumbed to the cold. The *Conchoderma* flowerlike barnacles had simply dropped off, while the ones that had dug in deeper, the *Panella* copepods, had died where they were and had had to be cast out by the whales' skin and blubber. Many of the canals the *Panella* had formed had become infected but as soon as those parasites were no longer living in them, the wounds had begun to heal. At the same time a number of small round green patches had begun to appear on the whales' bellies. Those would expand into a coating of minute antarctic plants almost like a fine moss. They would soon turn the whales' undersides green-yellow in color, for which the whaling men often called the blue whales sulphur bottoms. But these tiny plants would not cause any inconvenience. Except that the whales could observe them on one another, they would not have known they were there.

During that inactive period when the Whale's mother had been transferring her fat to him, he had become 50 feet long, nearly, but not quite, as large as he would have been if the two had been able to go ahead with their friends. By now, at the end of December, he should have been eating krill for more than two months and on that food he would have grown faster. At last, being out in the open sea, he could make a start toward finding the richer adult nourishment.

At the time he was born the Whale's tongue could discover that on his upper jaw there were rows of small parallel sheets, or leaves, of a horny material, almost as if he had had one continuous tooth all the way back on each side and it had somehow become cut into many thin crosswise slices. These hung down from his gums and were then about one inch long. They were not as rigid as true teeth would have been. When he ran the tip of his tongue along them he had been able to sway them, and he had learned that their inside edges were frayed out into fringes. Very curious; except that this baleen was a part of himself and therefore of course it felt normal.

The numerous sheets, with their fringy borders, were close together, only about half an inch apart, and they lengthened. They grew downward, so that now when the Whale was six months old they had become 16 inches long—effective strainers when there would be something on which to use them. And the sheets had spread inward. They, with their whiskery edges, covered all the roof of the Whale's mouth except for a ridge of palate along the center. The upper part of his mouth was filled with a hairy mass (actually made of the same sub-stance as hair, but coarse)—not a very appetizing thing for a tongue to be pushing around, one might think, but again, it was the Whale's own and so he was not repulsed by it.

One bright sunny morning he learned what this mouthful of hair was for, and at the same time he learned why he had under his throat 90 grooves which had been deepening and widening. He and his mother were swim-ming along through broken drift ice when, from a stretch of clear water head, the Whale heard a new sound like a wash of many small separate echoes. He swam faster and suddenly found himself drawing near to a swarm of krill, the shrimplike euphausids. In the same way that a school of fish or a flock of birds will wheel about all together, the krill swirled in unison, a spinning ball of live creatures now meaningful to the Whale. Instantly he had a new impulse to open his jaws very wide, an action which spread out the grooves, giving his mouth much more depth and allowing him to take in the swarm, take them all into his mouth along with the water in which they were swimming. Swiftly then he closed his mouth and the water drained out at the sides of his lips. Left behind, caught in the hairy fringes, were thousands of absolutely delicious morsels. The Whale knew, as well, what to do next. With his big mobile tongue he sucked the krill off his baleen and swallowed them—the first solid food that had ever gone into his stomach and utterly satisfying.

More! Where was more of that krill? He kept sending his signal out, right, left, straight ahead, and before long he heard the same murmur of tiny echoes. Another great mouthful—but no! It was his mother's turn and she had gulped in the swarm. As they went along then, day after day, they found more of the good food, the mother sometimes holding back so the young one could take it, at other times eating the krill herself.

Since southern blue whales ate almost nothing except the euphausids and on them achieved the greatest-ever animal bulk—a weight of 250,000 pounds and more —were these two-inch morsels, then, densely packed with nourishment? One would not think so to see them. For they were almost completely transparent, bits of pinkish jellylike nothing, little ghosts of beings. But nebulous though they were, they bore living lights so bright that six euphausids would illuminate a dark room well enough for human eyes to be able to read. And clever mites: the euphausids could flash their lights on and off at will, with two of the beams turning to focus on whatever their own eyes were seeing; and if they didn't like the look of it the euphausids would skip away. A crowd of them were a glow in the water, and also a hum, for they could produce sounds as well as flashing their lights. It took them two years to mature—complex, fascinating little creatures whose habits dominated the movements, the lives, of the greatest whales. And for all that they seemed to be made of light and air, they did contain carotene, which became Vitamin A in the whales' livers, perhaps one of the explanations for the whales' immense size.

Even so, krill seemed an unpromising meal for an animal like the young Whale; but soon he would be eating millions each day. And to sustain those numbers the krill themselves would consume untold amounts of plankton. The Antarctic is barren and inhospitable in the dark months when ice covers the sea, but in summer that great midwife, the sun, shines almost 24 hours a day and brings forth a wealth of minute plant life, ten times as abundant as that of the average in oceans elsewhere. The plankton animals grazing upon that harvest become the world's prototype of a population explosion. And as the final result: blue whales.

The north polar region, during the alternate half of the year, also has continuous daylight and sustains a great outburst of living. But there is no center of growth in the Arctic—or anywhere else—as rich as that surrounding South Georgia, because there is no other area which combines light with such beneficial winds, ocean currents and contours of seabed.

Under the southern sun the winds are ceaselessly blowing. Those from the east, in scouring the coast of the antarctic continent come to mountainous Graham Land, a long obstructing peninsula which extends north from the mass of earth and ice surrounding the Pole. The wind's force is caught in a pocket and gathering its energy turns northward along the peninsula.

As it streams ahead in its new direction, the wind whips up the Weddell Sea, stirring the waters all the way to the bottom. There they pick up great quantities of phosphates and nitrates, deposited on the ocean floor by the spent bodies of small marine animals. With this life-giving burden the Weddell Current follows the coast of Graham Land to its end and flows out into the Southern Ocean where it meets the West Wind Drift. With one giant surge the two currents sweep on toward South Georgia Island.

The island lies almost exactly east of Cape Horn. Between them is a spectacular drop from a higher sea-bed, a plunging cliff called the Scotia Arc. To the oncoming rush of waters it is a barrier with the island sitting on top. The island is crescent-shaped, surrounded by a flat shelf, submerged but shallow. The wall of the Arc, holding aloft its island, stands solidly against the besieging currents, but they divide and swing up and around the horns of the crescent. On the other, north side of the island then they slow down and spread out on the Shelf in an eddy. And there, having carried their nourishing silt all the way, the currents stir it around, keeping the minerals of the silt in motion, a natural fertilizer for the small plankton plants that feed the primitive animal life on which the blue whales grow so large.

There are other seas in which krill is found, but in quantities so much less that whales come from thousands of miles away to allay their hunger around South Georgia. Most of these particular whales will have gone without food for more than six months and here they fall to eating as though life depended on taking *this* immense mouthful, and then this, and this. The euphausids, only crumbs in size really, go down their throats in amounts that average three tons—6000 pounds—a day for each whale.

Since the season was near the height of the antarctic summer, the Whale and his mother encountered less and less ice as they drew near the island. They were finding some krill, still not enough to satisfy either whale, but their journey was nearly over. Finally they could feel a greater buoyancy in the water, for they were above a deep submerged trench and had more than five miles of ocean under them. The sensation of lightness was something the mother remembered, and she pressed ahead faster. At the end of the trench they faced a submarine cliff, the Scotia Arc, against which a strong current was surging. Giving themselves to it, they were carried up and out into shallow water, at last on the long-sought feeding grounds. Around them the krill was so dense that in places the two literally ate their way forward—not that they were eager to go any farther. They had come for this.

There were terrible dangers here, but for the present the instinct of self-preservation seemed to be better served by eating than keeping alert for whatever menace a whale might hear. One was audible but the two who had arrived so late were devouring in food as if no threat existed. Everywhere they turned the sea was luminous with krill and murmurous with their tiny voices. The whales gulped them in, nourishing, delectable food, all they could eat. The half-starved mother fed ravenously. The son's baleen, still only half as long as hers, did not trap the euphausids as well as hers did and sometimes it was just easier and more familiar to nudge his mother for milk, which she was even now willing to give him.

On all sides, it seemed, were whales—not as many as last year, not as many as had been here a month ago but far more than the numbers that would be left at the end of the hunting season, which still had three months to run. However small this gathering might seem to the Whale's mother, to him it was large, he had seen so few whales before. Fascinating were all the other great mouths opening and closing over swarms of euphausids. It was a pleasant rightness when they were other blue whales, although different kinds were more numerous. Fin whales: they were nearest to blues in size and there were more of them than any others. The young Whale could recognize them by their lopsided coloring. Humpbacks, also familiar: they were about as scarce as blues. Here they were not singing and not jumping out of the surface although they were lively below. Sperm whales: a band of those came by almost every day, en route to seas where they might find more squids. Plowing through krill with their great blunt heads, they could not feed here since they didn't have baleen in their mouths, only those long sharp teeth on their lower jaws and cavities above into which the teeth fitted. Finally the young one was seeing a species new to him—sei whales, straining out krill with baleen as he did, and almost exactly his length, soon to be 60 feet; but the seis seemed to be adults. Because they were fully grown it was legal to kill them, but not to kill the young blues until they were 70 feet long. The two species looked much alike except that the sei's color was grayer and the insignificant fins on their backs were slightly larger. If the human hunters were not to kill everything that swam they had to be able to identify a whale by such meager evidence as this and perhaps its spout, unless wind-scattered or mixed with spray, and decide instantly in the tumultuous waters whether the whale might be slaughtered. Not unnaturally mistakes were made. Anyway the crews had little interest in killing the smaller whales, which they called tiddlers.

Most of the blues the young Whale was seeing were his own size and age. Next in numbers, but they were thinning out rapidly, were the blues a year older. They were just over 70 feet long, vulnerable for the first time and not yet very skillful at dodging. The blues most scarce were the large adults like the Whale's mother, and one even was longer—100 feet. That whale and her mate were the first blues the two saw when they came up over the cliff and onto the island Shelf. The pair were idling along as they fed and except for a slight greeting as between blues, they did not stop for sociability. Mated pairs of blue whales were apt to be satisfied with the company of no more than each other and these two seemed absorbed in their bond as mates. The female was obviously pregnant. Already she had put on almost enough blubber to nourish herself, the fetus, and then an infant and one day soon no doubt she and her mate would be leaving here to go into warmer seas for the infant's birth—that is, if they escaped the hunters.

As she fed, the Whale's mother was leading the way along the edge of the Shelf to the northeast side where she knew the krill were likely to be most numerous and where the largest company of her own kind might be. Perhaps she was vaguely trying to find the four, including the mountain male, who had been so congenial as they approached Bouvet Island. Had they already been killed? All of them? She would search in the way an animal does—patiently turning this way and that, seeming obedient to a guide that gave only hints, an inner voice, intuition. And meanwhile she would continue to open her mouth upon the bright gatherings of krill, not neglecting to keep her son close to her here in this dangerous sea.

It was the Whale himself who discovered the young female who had been one of their traveling companions. She had gained so fast on her new nourishment that she was already four feet longer than he was. He would make up for his slow start but she would not know that and perhaps his backwardness put her off a bit, because the two brushed sides in a dense patch of krill and the Whale greeted her with a friendly interest but she did not respond. After they had exchanged clicks she started away. He followed her and his mother, seeking him, also found the young female and then her mother. The two adults were pleased to see each other. But where was the father and where was the mountain male? The mountain male might not have stayed with the others, but the father would have been with his family, surely, unless he had become one of the whalemen's victims—as he had. He had been killed the very day the family arrived at South Georgia.

The Whale, for all his driving need to eat, had times when the food here did not interest him. He always stopped feeding on krill for a while after he took in a mouthful of water that was nauseous with whales' blood. If he had been a carnivore, one that enjoyed eating mammalian flesh, the bloody water might have appealed to him, but a blue whale, feeding exclusively on his delicate fare of transparent small shrimps, would no more seek bloody flavors, especially the blood of his own kind, than he would kill the living animal, which would be inconceivable. When he and his mother passed through tainted water where a wounded whale had died a short time before, that was one of the occasions when he was apt to turn to her for her clean, comforting milk. But there was not always enough now. For there was a problem: her milk was drying up. She had nursed him for more than six months and that arrangement could not go on indefinitely.

Another reason his hunger lapsed was the deafening, crashing din, the bedlam of killing and cutting up whales. Prowling about over the island's Shelf were more than a hundred whale-catching boats, whose engines were always running and frequently the propellers turning—boats made of iron and steel which reverberated throughout the water with stinging sharpness. Since there had been ships near the African coast, the Whale had already heard the rumbling of engines and beat of propellers, but only of single ships. Faintly their sounds would approach, grow louder, diminish and die away, and though disturbing they had not been a danger. Here, besides the propellers and engines of boats very near, there were ships of gigantic size, stationary but causing the most harsh and piercing clamor—screechings, bangings and whine of immense steel cables, and worse: a hideous rending and tearing. Almost as shocking was the dull, crushing thud of exploding flesh when a harpoon struck its killing blow inside a whale's body. Living flesh does not normally explode, and when it did the sound was the voice of death itself.

At that time there were several whaling stations on the shore of South Georgia Island; each had a fleet of catcher boats and a factory to which the boats brought their victims. Larger in number and more deadly to whales were factory *ships* that could move around out in the sea and anchor wherever krill was abundant and therefore the whales were congregating. Nineteen of these factory ships were operating in the Antarctic that season and the majority had, as usual, stationed themselves at South Georgia. The ships were huge blunt iron boxes, 500 feet long, of up to 25,000 tons, nearly as large as airplane carriers, with crews of 700 men occupied in mincing, boiling and baking the bodies of whales. The ships were owned separately by whalemen of various nations, and each of the ships had its own fleet of a dozen or more catcher boats besides a few tow boats to collect the buoyed carcasses and bring them in to the factory ship. There the dead whales were taken on board up a slipway at the stern which sloped down into the water between the twin screws of the ship. But first the whales had to be killed.

The catcher boats were fast and maneuverable. Each

had a tall mast with a barrel on top for a lookout who kept peering over the sea for the feathery spray that meant the blow of a whale. He could recognize most of the spouts and when he cried out his information, what kind of whale, where it was and what way it was going, the boat sprang off after it.

In the prow was a swiveling gun manned by the boat's captain, who was always the gunner. He crouched over his weapon, intense, deadly skilled, ready to shoot when his victim had come within 50 yards. There were few failures. The gun sent a harpoon, with an explosive head and trailing a six-inch rope from the boat, deep into the whale's body. As soon as the whale, in his attempt to escape, put any strain on the rope the head exploded, causing four long barbs to open out, clutching into the whale's inner organs. After that any effort he made to get away simply tore greater wounds wherever the harpoon had lodged.

The most successful shot, bringing the quickest death, was placed to explode in a whale's chest, ripping into the heart or shattering the lungs. In that case the whale's next blow was a spout of blood, sometimes more than 20 feet high—"a chimney fire," the men called it, cheering because they had made a sure, fast kill. But the gunner must shoot from a heaving boat at a moving target, and so the harpoon often struck some less effective part of the whale's body and then there could be a long battle. A whale, unless instantly killed, usually sounded, going down very deep but trailing the rope attached to the harpoon inside him, and with a series of winches the crew would attempt to draw the whale up and close in for a killing shot with a second harpoon. This was not easy, for the whale would be fighting, lashing in and out of the water, vomiting, bleeding profusely, beating up tumults of ruddy spray and fiercely resisting the pull of the rope. And then the whale often chose to race away near the surface, sometimes dragging the 500-ton boat behind him even when its engines were set for full speed astern. The rope would be whipping the surface as he drew his attackers across the waves, incredibly with the harpoon barbs tearing farther and farther into him. The frantic thrust of his tail flukes would be heard throughout the sea and a thrashing as he beat the water in fury every time he was winched near the boat. The struggle could last a surprisingly long time, occasionally for hours if the great heart could hold out.

A far more humane method of killing whales had been invented: a harpoon with a lethal electric charge. But one whale believed to be dead had revived a little and caused some damage by flipping its tail while it was on the flensing deck of a factory ship. It would have been easy to avoid that possibility with a gunshot before the dead or stunned whale was brought into the ship. But the electrical weapon, cheaper, faster, more merciful, was abandoned. The fact that the crews preferred to continue the long, hideously cruel battles is not a comforting thought.

When a whale attacked with an explosive harpoon did finally die, the distribution of air and oil in his body would cause his carcass to turn over, belly uppermost. A hollow lance was thrust into his body and compressed air was pumped in to inflate it and keep it afloat—if it was that of a baleen whale; the dead toothed whales did not sink. Next, all but the stubs of the flukes were cut off, a custom that originated in the fact that there was a torque in the tail that could cause a whale's body to spin while it was being towed, whereupon even the strongest rope sometimes broke and snapping back, killed the tow-boat crew; but there was also a superstition that a dead whale with its flukes left on would swim away and be lost. After the flukes were discarded a notch was cut in the stump of the tail, identifying the catcher boat that had killed the whale and would be given a bonus for it; and finally a flagpole was driven into the upturned belly, with the ensign of the victorious company to signal its whereabouts to the tow boat. The kill was announced by radio to the factory ship and the catcher boat left to continue its search for more whales.

Until the tow boat arrived the waves rocked the buoyed carcasses, bodies of shy, reticent creatures whose light-colored underbellies looked pitifully naked. The compressed air caused the grooves on the throats to spread apart, a female's nipples to come out of their folds, and sometimes a male's penis to extrude. The penis of a blue whale was six to eight feet long and it was considered amusing to make golf bags out of them.

A tow boat could bring in as many as seven dead whales at a time. These were moored behind the factory ship to be dragged one by one up the slipway to the decks where the work was done—out of sight but not out of hearing. For the sounds from the factory ship were louder and even more gruesome than the explosions of flesh—the violations were so gigantic. First there were an unbelievable crashing and clanging as an enormous steel claw—called the grab—was dropped down and clamped onto the stump of the tail. And then, with a great rattle

and whir, chains and winches pulled the whale, perhaps weighing 100 tons or more, tailfirst to the flensing platform. For a few moments there was relative quiet as teams of flensers made long cuts through the whale's skin and blubber, from nose to tail. Hooks were implanted and then followed unearthly shrieks as the immense strips of blubber were quickly torn from the bodies by winches. In the ripping away of the blubber, mute flesh found a voice, screaming its protest at having all of its living, its growing and later sustaining life, so brutally peeled away. There had never been any sounds like these before in the history of the earth, for there had never been, anywhere, such monstrous killings.

Finally there was the clamor of ratcheting saws dismembering the head, vertebrae and other bones. The entire carcass was disposed of in a factory at the rate of one every 30 minutes: only that long for all the whale, so recently moving through its element with consummate grace, to be chopped up and dispersed into vats and ovens. Except that every few hours there was a recess so that the men could wash their greasy, bloody hands and sit down and eat lunch, a meal often of whale meat. But occasionally there was one who found that he wasn't hungry, who instead went outside, away from the stench, under a sky spread with the fresh and innocent saffron, rose and ethereal blue of a polar summer.

7

A Choice of Deaths

Whales and men were not the only life at South Georgia. The same kind of elephant seals were here that had been at Bouvet but they were not at this season interestingly fighting and mating. They were out in the waves, very lean, with their coats looking too big for them, but they were eating squids on which they would soon fatten up. And something new to the Whale: flocks of birds so dense they almost covered the sea. Men said there were millions of them, crowding around floating whale carcasses and the huge intestines, the only part of a dead whale that was cast overboard from the factories.

Riding the surface, however filthy, were the patchwork-colored Cape pigeons, pintado petrels actually but with plump bodies like pigeons; and the romantic wandering albatrosses which often ate so much that they couldn't rise from the water, not even on wings that spread to a width of 11 feet. More fastidious were the Wilson's petrels, dancing above the waves, only wetting their toes as their beaks snatched up morsels. Dominion gulls were there too, adding shrill cries to what was a pandemonium.

But the birds that always astonished the Whale were the gentoo penguins. They obviously were birds because they *flew*—but under water! They had narrow wings which moved as birds' did when they soared up from the surface, wings with the same kind of stroke though slower than that of the airborne birds, but so powerful! Miniature creatures less than a twentieth the length of the Whale at that time, yet they could fly through the sea faster than the Whale could swim, unless possibly he were making a dash for life. And the penguins did their submerged flying in flocks, just as other birds flew in the air. Twenty-five, fifty of them would suddenly sweep past the Whale or even his mother when they were cruising along at a whale's normal speed. Disconcerting, a little, when blue whales were supposed to be supreme in the sea. The penguins appeared to eat krill but that didn't bother the Whale. There was enough for everyone.

He was getting all his own food by late February and was starting to have a sense of self-sufficiency, a recognition, intuitive no doubt, that he belonged to the largest, strongest, fastest species of animals in the ocean (fastest except for penguins). He would never be arrogant because that was not the way of blue whales, but quietly confident he would assume his superior rank. Already he knew that he no longer needed to fear killer whales. Some of those were here on the Shelf, ignoring most other whales except the ones that were dead. They did eat the head parts of buoyed carcasses when they were not towed away quickly, and along with the birds they scavenged the discarded whale intestines. In any case the Whale had already proved to himself that he could swim faster than killer whales and so he had no more fear of them. If they should attack he could get away.

But the Whale was not, after all, supreme—for there were men. He was having great difficulty in learning that they were enemies. True, he saw the whale carcasses but he did not see any of those tiny animals, men, actually battling with a whale and it was not in his inherited instincts to understand distance killing.

No one had yet sent a harpoon toward him or his mother, for this precise reason: that they were usually together. They were therefore known to be a nursing mother and infant. Killing either of those was one of the strongest—though not always observed—prohibitions of that gathering of men who called themselves the International Whaling Commission. Originally their purpose was to allow a young whale to live until he could reproduce himself, and mothers were necessary until he outgrew his need for milk. But that regulation was simply one of those meaningless gestures that groups of men often make, because it allowed a young whale to be killed as soon as he or she was 70 feet long, which was two or three years before the age when the blue whales would mate. Their age at sexual maturity had been proved by careful studies of the testes of dead males and the ovaries of dead females, and the proof was that they did not bear young until they were well over the 70-foot length. But the earlier rule was allowed to stand and so the whale-men went on shooting the 70-foot youths, depriving themselves of a new generation of blue whales that could have kept the stocks of this most valuable species continuing into the future. The Whale's mother was being logical in her sense of doom, for the year that her son first went to the South Georgia feeding grounds there were only enough blues there for the whalemen to take one on an average in every four days—22 altogether. Twenty-five years earlier, 17,000 blues had been killed at the island in one season.

The Whale himself might be safe this year, since he was still 12 feet under the crucial 70-foot length. And as long as he appeared to be in the nursing phase, that is, as long as his small spout kept rising close to his mother's tall one, she probably was safe too. But he was not staying so close to her now. On his own initiative he was investigating those fascinating objects, the catcher boats, and he was playing more and more often with two new friends, orphaned youths of his own species. His absence made his mother more vulnerable.

At the Whale's first underwater sight of a catcher boat he had found that its keel resembled the keel of a fish—perhaps of a monstrous dorado, swimming along as dorados do, partly out of the surface? But the propeller: the strangest tail ever. As one of the boats passed over him he discovered that the boat's tail fins went around and around. He never had seen any tail of a fish or whale do that, and he followed the object for a short way until his mother came and severely nudged him off to the side and then into a dive. But the Whale's curiosity was not satisfied. He kept wanting to swim up close to one of those spinning tails. Should he touch it? Maybe not. His mother tried to convince him that she wished him to stay away from the boats but he still was inquisitive.

So too was the Indian Ocean female, the young one, although her mother was even more determined to teach her that boats could be deadly. The young orphaned blues were not forbidden to go near the boats, since all their parents were dead, and those two gave the crews plenty of chance to kill them. Perhaps they were not harpooned for the very reason that the men had such a good opportunity to know they were undersized. It was much easier to estimate a whale's length at five or ten yards than the usual 50 yards at which gunners shot. And the youthful pair were in fact so fearless that the men came to recognize them individually, partly by their *Cyamus* scars. Protected by their smallness they played around the boats, for neither was quite 60 feet long as yet, the length they would reach at the end of their first season here. Meanwhile they were acquiring a confidence in the boats and men that could be dangerous for them in the following year when they would be of a size it was legal to slaughter.

Before they had killed any whale the men had an almost certain knowledge of what they were getting. They knew first from the spouts: a high straight shaft from an adult blue whale; one shorter but also slender would be a fin whale's; a humpback's was lower and widely spread and that of a sperm whale came out of the side of his head and projected forward. Wind that dispersed the spouts and disguising spray from a breaking wave could cause doubt, but the men gathered other signs in the brief time a whale was in sight. They noted the skin color and the position and size of the slight fin toward the end of the back. As a whale turned down in his dive, all his back emerged like a rotating wheel, allowing the men to estimate very well what his total length was. And the men were sharp.

Sometimes it was tempting to get the young ones even though they might yield little more than a ton of oil, especially tempting late in the season when most of the larger whales had been caught. Before a dead whale was cut up on the factory ship, it was supposed to be seen by an official who accompanied every whaling expedition and was obligated to report any illegal catches. His judgment was seldom questioned and an offending gunner might be sent to jail back home for several months. But that lone official had to associate with hundreds of crew members, most of whom cared only for the bonus they got for each kill. A tense conflict of interest lasted for the eight months of a trip to the Antarctic, during which great animosities could build up, especially considering the crowded quarters and the revolting work. And so it happened at times that the observer was absent somewhere on the ship when a whale obviously too small or a female with swollen mammary glands was brought in. He did not stay away frequently, but often enough so that no whale on the feeding grounds was safe, whatever its size or condition.

The adult blues knew that they were the whales in the greatest danger, because any catcher boat that was chasing a different kind of whale would give up that pursuit and take after a blue it had sighted. But the blue whales were clever—quick-witted, the men called them. They always turned after they knew they had been seen so that they didn't come up the next time in the same direction they had been heading. They might reverse or streak off to right or left, or most often zigzag—do anything except what a man on a boat might expect. And this shrewdness was so frustrating to gunners that they became more determined than ever to get the elusive blue whales, not only because they produced 80 barrels of oil —nearly twice as much as a fin whale, its nearest in yield —but also because the men felt themselves challenged. There was prestige as well as an extra bonus in killing a blue.

The movements of boats and the cunning of the men were of course well known under the water. No boat ever crept up unsuspected near a blue whale that had risen to blow. But the spout of a whale could be seen at some distance, the lookouts kept searching on all sides, and if a valuable whale was seen behind a boat the boat would swing around in pursuit. And where would a whale, once discovered, surface next time? It was the normal way of most kinds of whales to swim along in a fairly straight line, but the experienced blues had learned not to do that when they had been observed. The Whale's mother taught him, by showing that these things were her habit, to blow as far away from the boats as possible when he ran out of breath, and then to proceed on some unpredictable course. There was a desperate need to keep always out of the range of those guns on the forward decks of the boats.

Finding her son one time with his head out of the

water to look at a boat, but not in immediate danger because he was behind it, she rushed forward to topple him with a ramming so hard that it hurt for the rest of the day. Afterward he became more obedient and began following her example and avoiding the boats.

And then, before long, the Whale learned unforgettably why they were dangerous. He and his mother were swimming away from one of them when another approached their path. They were not quite close enough yet for the gunner to try a shot and they were getting out of the way very fast when an amazing thing happened: they heard the voice of the mountain male for the first time here on the Shelf and realized that he must have recognized them, for he was coming their way. He was sweeping ahead and continuing to call in that poignant voice they could remember. The mother and her son with her slowed ever so slightly. Her voice answered the male's. This was going to be a most welcome reunion—the male apparently thought so too, for his call rose in pitch. An eagerness had come into it.

They were all under the surface and it seemed safe to slow down still further. A tremor was flickering through her body. But when he was only a length away, the male came up to the top to take a quick breath. The other two saw him rise and immediately start to submerge again when, with a hideous blasting sound, his whole body seemed to explode. Up into the air and all through the water went flesh, geysers of blood and great chunks of bone. He must be attempting to dive, for his head has turned down but the rest of his body does not follow into a dive, since his spine has been shattered and he cannot control his flukes. A thick rope is trailing out of his cavernous wound. It draws tight and, as a last agonized cry escapes from the dying whale, the boat's winches begin to turn, pulling the victim closer for the macabre ritual of being filled with compressed air and buoyed for the tow boat.

The mother and son had sped away, the young Whale following her lead without question, sensing his need for her guidance, now with the knowledge that comes to all animals who encounter men who are killers. Now he knew the meaning of those explosions that sent unnatural vibrations through the waves, now he knew why the water he took into his mouth sometimes tasted of whale blood, now he understood that the upside-down whales lying so still at the surface were dead. All these meanings assembled in an emotion he had not felt since he was an infant: fear. If men had not come into their lives adult blue whales might have been almost unique among animals in not being acquainted with fear. Since only a brief time ago in their history they have known it, however. Fear, dread, insecurity and hence caution: the blue whales were developing these but such qualities were not natural to them. They were not yet inborn but the whales' consciousness had enlarged to take in the new dangers. And sadly they might be pushing out what had been the innate temperament of blue whales.

With the chance of continuing life, for an individual blue whale or his offspring, coming to seem so slight, it would not be strange if the relationship between blue-whale mates failed to progress from affection to sex. It had come to this impasse in numerous species who ceased to reproduce when all the circumstances, except for an overwhelming menace, seemed favorable. Still enough food and homesites, good enough health, the traditional species habits that formerly led to pairing: all these intact, but the final impulse not there any longer. The young Whale might reach that crucial point soon, might find a friend who would be a congenial companion—but to go further? It was a turning he might have to make before long. The way opening to the future: would it be yes or no?

South Georgia, directly east of Cape Horn, received the full impact of the Horn's weather, recognized by everyone as the most violent in the world. When the westerly wind of the South Pacific hits the very high Andes mountain range, it is deflected southward to and around Cape Horn, the tip of the South American continent. There it is almost always of gale or hurricane strength. Beyond the Horn that wind meets no obstruction for 1000 miles, until it reaches South Georgia lying diagonally across its path.

The Whale didn't know it because he could not see that far, but South Georgia Island was a ridge of very high snow-covered mountains. He did experience the effects of that ridge. For it turned the Cape Horn winds so that sometimes they came whipping around the northwest corner of the steep, oblique barrier, and then, often within fifteen minutes, around the opposite southeast corner. The two conflicting winds vented their force on the waters over the Shelf. These waters, being shallow, were hurled upward without much resistance from beneath. Towering waves that ran ahead of the northwest gale were apt to meet those of a southeast gale, the result being stupendous watery chaos. In the antarctic autumn beginning in March the winds often blew at 100 miles an hour and besides driving up waves that seemed mountain-high, the winds lifted whole sheets of water which sailed through the air as if the sea's surface had taken swift, level flight.

Unless, then, the autumn storms came late, March was the month when the factory ships and their catcher boats had to flee back to the island coast for shelter, most of the catcher boats to be tied up there in the coves for winter, the factory ships to wait for a break in the terrible weather so they could make a dash out of this maelstrom into quieter seas for the voyage home with their cargos.

The whales did not fear the waves. It was somewhat tiring to try to make progress through them, but the whales could swim at lower depths except when they rose to blow. There was an inconvenience in the way the turbulence scattered the krill. It broke up the larger rafts of euphausids although small aggregates sometimes stayed together—if one could find them. The whales, relieved of the threats from the catcher boats, might therefore remain a little longer here on the feeding grounds for some last meals before ice covered the waters, and the krill, over the Shelf. By then, the whales would be gone.

Ice, if broken enough, was no novelty to them and would not drive them away. Ice fields were always descending the slopes of the island and frequently broke when they reached the shore, casting off icebergs. In the tempestuous waters these were smashed up rather fast, great masses as large sometimes as the factory ships being hurled about, scattering smaller chunks. The men in the boats were more alarmed by these than the whales were.

The first year the Whale was there the autumn storms started the third week in March. They impelled all the ships and boats to give up for that season. Each of the catcher captains hoped and tried, however, to appear with a good number of final whale carcasses—bring them in themselves rather than calling by radio for the tow boats. And one of these captains, the Scot who had hunted most persistently near the edge of the Shelf where the Whale and his mother fed, had special reasons for wanting to end with a record catch. Therefore he made an almost demoniacal search the last day before he left. No matter that his fairly small boat stood on end as it met each wave, no matter that his crew were more than ready to call it a season, and no matter that towing a large pod of whales to the factory would be an almost impossible task in these seas: he was a stubborn man.

He was one of the whalemen who were planning to buy farms or ranches when they retired, and this was his last year at South Georgia. Many, if not most, had the same ambition. During the long months in the Antarctic, it had been remarked often, almost the whole conversation on the ships was about cattle and horses. For those, not crops, were what most of the men were planning to raise. It seemed that being associated with whales for as many as 30 years in some cases, the men felt something like an affinity for animals. They were killing the great wild ones in order to make money enough to involve themselves with smaller, passive, domesticated creatures. Some of the men were already buying their farms. The Scot had already done so. His wife and son had been running his farm for several years, but next year he expected to be there himself and by taking over the management of it, he hoped to increase the farm's profits. He was still thinking of money as well as animals. If he should take in a pod of seven adult blue whales at the end of this day he would earn, besides his salary, $210 and with that he would put a new fence around his upper pasture. Staring into blank walls of water, hour after hour on that last day, a vision of his hillside pasture was continually near the surface of his mind. With the profits from this year's whaling he knew, for sure, he could pay off the mortgage. Luck should be with him now: his hopes were so high, they would create it, although he did recognize that seven blue whales was too many to be considered likely. Well then, *some* blue whales—a few fin whales, of which there were more left here than blues, and at the very end of the day, if necessary, a couple of little seis. Meanwhile, he was plowing through the gigantic waves, knowing that the violent water would be making the sea below very noisy for whales and so they might not hear his boat as clearly as if the weather had been more calm. He accepted the storm as the challenge that he must meet in order to take in his seven whales.

He was immensely encouraged when the first whale killed, and not long after dawn (when she probably felt protected by the faintness of the light), was the pregnant female who had been here with her mate ever since the Whale and his mother arrived. The Scottish captain was elated, for he estimated that she was 100 feet long and obviously was fat—whether pregnant or not, he could not know. It would have been a supreme piece of luck if the female had had a devoted mate who would also have fallen prey to the gunner's harpoon. Briefly the Scot thought he did glimpse another large whale in the depths, but the female had been killed instantly with a shot square in the lungs, and so the mate, if that's who it was, did not stay around.

With such a good start even the crew were encouraged. They buoyed the female and set out to look for more whales.

For several hours they did not see or catch any others. And then, shortly after noon a pair of fin whales rose in the crest of a nearby wave. The gunner got one immediately and an hour later, shooting a second fin, he thought he had killed the other. Although it was only a fin, killing it gave him some special satisfaction. He was always angry when a whale he hoped to catch got away. And so whether the second fin was the mate of the first or not, he preferred to believe it was.

Now he had three and his mind turned again to blues. He went back near the edge of the Shelf, which could be detected by the form of the waves breaking over the deeper water; that was where he had got the first female blue—perhaps others were here.

He was right! A second large female went down to his gun. It was the Indian Ocean mother and though the Scot searched the surrounding water, no mate was in sight—naturally, because he had already slaughtered that mate several months before. But this female did not die quickly. The harpoon had entered her side, behind her flipper, one of the worst spots for a gunner who hoped to make a fast kill. And then while she fought, here to confound the situation came an immature female, her daughter apparently from the way the young one kept fearlessly swimming close to the other, reversing roles, it seemed, the small one giving sympathy to the mother.

There followed one of the truly hideous episodes of the whaling oceans. For the gunner, beside himself with exasperation, shot the daughter but she was not killed immediately either, and now he would just have to play the two of them until both died of exhaustion.

The young one was the more desperately wounded, and so now it was the mother who made an effort to be close to her, to give encouragement, urging her to escape. Though the sea was rough the thrashing of the two whales, their spinning and churning, plunging dives and explosive surfacing created their own waves, and with bleeding from both the whales, the sea became a red froth. The Scot was tempted to cut one of the victims loose but, stubborn in all situations, he held onto them. Hour after hour passed. The young one was first to die. She had seemed to be blinded by pain for she turned one way and another, often toward the boat. Pitifully she swam about on the surface and her mother, clumsily and off-balance, tried to get under her to ride her away. But finally the immature whale gave up and with only a few last flutters died. Her mother died also then, and the two were buoyed side by side as they often had lain in life, with the daughter seeming very small since her mother's body was more than 30 feet longer.

Now the Scot had five whales. Full daylight was long past but the scene was not entirely dark for there was a moon, although clouds often hid it. The men in the catcher boat continued to hunt. Dawn came again. Twenty-four hours had passed since the pregnant female was killed. She should have been taken up into the factory ship by now. Thirty-three hours from death was the

cut-off time, for beyond that period the oil was not supposed to be usable. But exceptions were sometimes
made. And since this was the Scot's last trip he could
hope for leniency. But he could not wait much longer.

Up and down over the waves rode the boat. The
crew had been cheered by some generous portions of
rum but they were tired and becoming impatient. The
captain, the gunner, was beginning to consider the
thought that he should get his buoyed carcasses in line for
a tow to the ship. That would be defeat, in a way, because
he always liked to meet any aim he had set for himself.
He thought of it as a point of honor.

And he was, after all, to catch his seven. For a group
of sei whales came by; it was legal to kill them even
though they were short, inasmuch as they were adult.
The guns had been loaded again after buoying the blue
whale mother and daughter, and it was not a great trick
to kill two of the seis, exactly as he had anticipated, for
—perhaps being stimulated by the violent storm—they
did not seem normally wary. Now, 32 hours after killing
the pregnant female, the crew proceeded to fasten chains
around the stumps of the tails and attach them to the stern
of the boat. This load would not be a great triumph but
it was a small one. The Scot persuaded himself that he
was satisfied.

The pregnant female was the last to be worked on.
She looked bloated, the captain saw. More than compressed air had fattened her. Gases from internal decom-
position were building up inside her, as he had to recognize. No matter. No time to think about anything but
getting on the way back with his pod of whales. He
would probably be the last catcher boat in for this season,

and applause, praise would be awaiting him at the ship. One overripe female, a huge one, would be forgiven, and also the illegal small daughter. Those things happened. There were seldom penalties when the offenses came on the final day.

The crew, feeling their rum, wet to the skin with icy water and tired from the frenzied activity of more than 30 hours, were not at their sharpest in assembling the carcasses. They were having special difficulties in lining up the pregnant whale's body on the outside of the others. At the rail the gunner-captain shouted directions against the roaring wind. A wave lifted the carcass to the height of the deck; for a minute it seemed as if it would swim aboard. The bloating had increased so much that the captain actually thought of cutting her loose. As two of the crew, then, were manipulating the tow chain around her tail, the fetus inside her, weighing more than two tons, was expelled by the pressure within. It shot out of her, all that weight, so fast that the captain did not have time to dodge. But he never knew what had happened, for the fetus struck his head, knocking it quite off his shoulders and hurling it into the waves. The crew stood in their places, frozen with shock, while the fetus drifted away, as did the head briefly. The men in the boat did not have a chance to recover it, for it sank. When they could move again they carried the headless body of their captain to his cabin and laid it on his bunk and then, some of them frankly weeping, they started the boat on their terrible trip through the storm back to the factory ship. But first they cut the overripe carcass away, since they knew it would have no value.

Two of the crew had seen the startling expulsion of

an unborn whale from the body of its mother, but it had happened on the flensing platform of a factory ship where the flensers were always aware of that possibility and stayed out of range. It was more liable to happen there, after a carcass was near or over the 33-hour legal delay and was full of gases. Usually the catcher boats were only involved with carcasses for a short time after the killing. The death of the captain in this case had been due to his eagerness to take in as big a haul as possible, waiting beyond the sensible time.

The mother of the fetus lost most of the compressed air when the fetus burst out of her, and by morning there was no sign of her or her nearly born young one—except in the depths. As she sank the luminescent plankton made her look almost alive, and so did the descending fetus and the head of the captain, whose hair trailed streamers of light. For a short way the Whale and his two new friends followed them down.

The mate of the pregnant female was numbed by his loss, and a few days after her death he left the island to start the journey back to his own summer sea, which was near Saint Helena Island. The Whale's mother left too. There was not any recognized pair bond between them; they were just two lonely whales each finding a little comfort in another blue's company. The mother knew that her son was due to leave her, and she had enough blubber now to see her through to the next feeding season. There was no reason to stay and a slight reason to go, and so she went.

The Whale and his two young friends formed a trio.

They stayed at South Georgia long enough to eat some more krill and were no longer vulnerable. They were saved by the savage weather and the fact that the catcher boats had given up for the season. They continued their feasting for a few more weeks while the storms followed one after another so closely that a whale could not tell them apart.

The three were gradually making their way to the northwest side of the Shelf. When they reached it they swam across the open sea to the Falkland Islands, near Patagonia. There they would turn north along the South American coast—a route the orphaned pair knew because they had come south that way with their parents in the previous autumn. The Whale, a little behind them in development because he had not had a chance to eat as much krill, was quite willing at this early stage to have them guide him. And with his buoyant and still playful nature he was welcomed as a companion by the others— all of them full of youthful high spirits as they started toward whatever adventures lay ahead while they continued their growing up.

8

Where the Wild Ones Were

After their months of strenuous eating, the three young whales could wander about with a freedom almost unknown to any creatures on earth except baleen whales. Even the toothed whales, the sperms, killers, dolphins and others, must continue to feed all year and travel about to find their preferred kind of nourishment. But the trio could now forget all that bother. Food to last them at least for six months was stored in their blubber and so all they had to do now was mature—to discover what their particular world was like, and how to fit themselves into it. Had all the dangers been concentrated

127

around South Georgia or would there be others that they must learn to avoid without parents' protection? They would soon know; and after six months they must find krill again, no doubt in the midst of human hunters. But now forward into the prospect of carefree enjoyment!

Their northbound traveling was assisted by a tongue of north-flowing water, the Falkland Current. The whales splashed along in it, heading for a sea of more comfortable warmth but no doubt with only a vague impression that they would find it. It came to meet them. While the Falkland Current was still running strong it burst into the south-flowing Brazilian Current, composed of water from near the Equator and therefore deliciously warm. After the two currents came together they both swung east, out into the South Atlantic, and where they collided the whales had some fun, for the impact caused an immense chop, great peaks of water rising here and there, no one could say where next, and the mix below the surface was a delightful chaos. The whales allowed themselves to be tumbled about, as playful as infants, but gradually worked along toward the north where the flow was all peaceful and soothing. The whales enjoyed this too, in its different way.

But there was a group of sea mounts ahead, cones rising up from the seabed to near the surface, and the trio nearly ran into one that came to within 15 feet of the top. The Whale himself, who was a short way in advance of the others, had a fright when a rocky slope appeared less than his own length in front of him. He swung sharply off to the right and his friends, hearing his clicks' sudden accelerando, were warned and followed him. This was the kind of emergency that parents had watched for till recently; now the young ones must be more wary. They must not plunge ahead recklessly. They would learn.

Soon they came into a wide warm pool in the ocean, a space clear of obstructions more than three miles deep over a seabed that men called the Pernambuco Abyssal Plain. The three felt the buoyancy and dived, chasing each other up and down, sensing their safety. The South Equatorial Current flowed through the upper layers of water, and since it came all the way from that similar pool off the African coast, the Angola Basin, some of the same kinds of creatures were here and the Whale felt a similarity something like home. The three would stay for a while.

For by now they were in their own world, again in the world where only the wild ones were. At last they were far from South Georgia, from the sound and sight of those curious and distressing animals, men. But men were not quite forgotten. Nothing so strange, so alarming could go out of the Whale's memory in the few weeks since he had started north.

The connection between the men on the boats and the deaths of whales was not clear, but undoubtedly it existed.

Even apart from the deaths, men were disturbing. They looked like animals but they did not act in animals' normal ways. They had no grace. Their motions did not flow one into another as whales' motions did, or fishes', or sharks'. As the Whale had seen men on the decks of the catcher and tow boats, and working on the dead whales, the men's motions had seemed unnatural, not relaxed and easy nor yet smoothly impulsive as wild animals' motions were. Whales, any animals, judged other

animals by their motions: did they show fear or aggressiveness, were other animals tense or resting? Motions
were language but no one could understand those of
men.

There was a hardness—those arms stabbing forward
—even when otherwise men did not seem to attack.
There was a hardness and suddenness in everything that
they did. Did they not know that small vulnerable creatures like themselves should try to avoid being noticed?
They should be humble, be quiet, and always be ready
to disappear instantly.

If a whale ever saw a man down in the sea he could
ram him and kill him. He could—but would he? Probably not. Whales did not kill for no reason. Besides, there
was some barrier: what? This was the most confusing of
all the impressions the men had made. There was a kind
of zone of safety surrounding men. It would not seem
right to a whale to kill them. To kill would be difficult
because something would prevent. Fear of men? Not
exactly. Just a prohibition that apparently did not apply
to any other animals except men. Why did it apply to
them? Because their minds had a unique power of
thought, a quality that some animals might not recognize;
but the Whale, who did, still could not analyze it. Better
to watch this shark. He too was acting strangely, writhing
about that way. What was happening to him?

Sharks and killer whales were alike in being dangerous to infant blues, but no longer: since the Whale could
now swim faster than they could or he could ram one that
attacked, he did not need to fear them and the sharks and
killers knew that too and made no threatening moves.
But this shark that was flinging himself about here as in

pain: why was he doing that? Soon the Whale saw the skin, then the flesh break in the side of the shark and the face of a fish appeared in the opening. Its mouth chewed away the edge of the hole until there was space enough for the whole fish to break through. It was a porcupine fish *(Diodon antennatus),* the same prickly kind the infant Whale had seen off the coast of Africa, a fish that could blow itself up with a supply of air and water on which it might survive long enough to eat its way out of an enemy's stomach. That it had done alone there in the dark of the shark's flesh, and the Whale saw it finally emerge into freedom and swim away. It was small by then, with most of its air and water used up, and its exit looked like a grotesque birth, only of course that it came out of the wrong place; and the shark died of its wound.

Interesting to the Whale because he had not seen one before was a green turtle, a creature enclosed in a horny box. She had legs, or at least feet, with which she was paddling ahead through the waves. Strange, in this element where whales, sharks and fish were as fluently sinuous as the water itself, the green turtle was one without grace. But she did seem sure of herself as she plodded along in her resolute way, and no wonder, for unknown to the Whale of course, she had just done a tremendous thing.

Finding a place on the beach where the sand was fine and soft, she had gone ashore, had climbed away from the water, up above the high-tide line, dragging a body that weighed several hundred pounds. Laboriously, slowly she continued, all the time making a track in the sand that soon would defeat her efforts.

Having come to a spot where the sand was warm

and just right, she had dug a deep hole and squatting above it had dropped a clutch of smooth, almost round eggs into it. Then she had shoveled sand over the eggs, filling the hole and after smoothing the sand skillfully, she had gone back to the sea, her year's project completed.

The eggs would never hatch there. No lively little turtles would dig their way out of the sand and scamper down to the water where, pitting their tiny strength against the buffeting waves, they would begin a life in the ocean. For almost as soon as the mother was gone, two men, each with a bucket, would find the track she had made and follow it to the well-disguised nest and take the eggs, which they would hatch in an incubator, and as soon as the young turtles were large enough would sell them to be made into canned green turtle soup. It happened every year, and the mother had never known.

But even her effort was small compared with that of some other green turtles here off the South American coast. Following an inbred tradition they swam all the way out to Ascension Island to lay their eggs. Those too would be dug up as regularly.

Where was there a shore that no men had found, that still belonged to the wild ones, who might still live there and play and mate and raise their young ones unharmed?

The Whale might have had such thoughts if he had known about green-turtle soup, but to him the mother was just a neighbor and her ways, though unusual, were obviously wild and so she was another that he accepted as rightfully here in this wild world that he had discovered. It was so truly his natural world that he had no reason, yet, to suspect that it didn't exist everywhere except at South Georgia.

As the days passed in these pleasant waters and the three young ones continued their growth, it developed gradually that the Whale, even though slightly the smallest, was the one with a strong sense of leadership. It was a quality little understood by men, but they recognized it and knew that it could appear, unexplained, in certain individual animals; and if the species were one of the social ones, the natural leader took the initiative in whatever he and his associates did. The two orphans did not resent the Whale's more decisive temperament. They were content to follow. And so, when the Whale became bored in this Pernambuco pool and wanted to see what was farther north, the trio set out again.

Soon they approached the Equator but never quite reached it. What stopped them? It seemed to be an invisible boundary. North of it they would have found a population of blues who were almost identical but who, for their part, stayed on the opposite side: a mysterious separation.

Those of the Northern Hemisphere also migrated into a colder ocean for their annual feeding, going up into the Arctic. Those blues had the same habit as that of the southern whales, of eating for half a year and then resting, playing, courting, and bearing young during the alternate half, when they too would be in the mild placid ocean near the Equator—but never crossing it. The northern blues appeared to be just like the southerners except that they weren't quite as large—for the reason, men thought, that the arctic plankton was not as nourishing as the krill in the South. It was not as plentiful either, nor concentrated in any one place as the food at South Georgia was.

Why didn't the two populations—blues of the North and those of the South—meet and mingle along the Equator? Doubtless because of their timing. By early May when the southerners would be coming into the sub-Equatorial waters, the northern whales would be on their way to the Arctic, and the same kind of lapse would keep them apart in the autumn. There was never a question of southerners like the trio proceeding on up to the Arctic after they reached the Equator because they would have already acquired their year's quota of food. There would seem to be better reason for the less well-fed whales from the North to continue on to South Georgia and perhaps become permanent southerners, but as far as men knew none of them ever did. This was an unusual situation in nature—two populations of the same species having a mutual borderline but not intermingling. It brings up questions that fascinate zoologists: about how the two groups became separated; was there a time in the past when they were all one, perhaps soon after whales came away from the land to live in the ocean? And when and in what part of the world was that? No fossil whale bones had ever been found—only the vestigial, now useless bones in the flippers and flanks telling that whales had once walked. They still grow in the bodies of both southern and northern blues, but the rest of the story is silence.

This part of the sea where the whales were loafing was near the doldrums, and some of the trash from that stagnant area was drifting about. The whales would have liked to play and doze at the surface, as blues often did when they came into idle waters, but they had to lie here among blobs and clumps of oil, plastic spoons and dishes and rubber sandals and bathing caps. The oil was the worst; it got into their eyes, and once when the Whale was breathing in oxygen a polythene bag got sucked into one of his blowholes. With his next spout it came out again, but the whales, with a joint impulse, left and swam southward again into that pleasant Brazilian Current. In some stretches along near the coast they came into polluted water and taking a gulp of plankton into their mouths, they took in the flavor of chemicals or of human waste, but that was not something they did very often, since their kind of food was not in this part of the ocean.

In their wanderings the trio found most amusement back in the junction of the two opposed currents, the Falkland and the Brazilian. Not only was there a lively tumbling of waters but this was a gathering place for whales of many kinds and it was diverting to be among them—at least if one belonged to the largest species and therefore had nothing to fear. Killer whales were here; they attacked dolphins and smaller porpoises and occasionally a humpback, too slow to get out of their way. But the killers left the three blues alone.

At this point on the coast that great river, La Plata, entered the sea. It brought nutrients on which plankton thrived; these nourished a large population of fishes and squids; and that food attracted the toothed whales such as sperms and dolphins. Some of the baleen whales here would strain out a few mouthfuls of plankton from time to time but it wasn't the kind they liked—they had joined the others because they enjoyed the merry waves and the sociability.

Congenial and entertaining were a large company of pilot whales (*Globicephala melaena,* sometimes called blackfish)—160 of them, a herd that was actually a harem. They looked a little like killer whales, being almost as long, also black except, in this southern species, a flash of white on the sides of their heads—as the killers had. But their bulging, globe-shaped foreheads (sadly heads that would be their doom) distinguished them from the killers, as did their playfulness. Since they lived on squids and fish they had no urge to slaughter warm-blooded animals, and lacking a hunter's always intense bloodthirsty appetite, they could squander the days in rollicking pleasure.

This was a nuptial festivity, and what a splashing and lobtailing and leaping out of the water it was! Also a vocal clamor, chirping, whistling and calls back and forth, five different kinds of sounds that were obviously joyous. The herd master, a strong mature male, was having a riotous time. The waves were churned into foam, and the blues on the edge of the harem, themselves young and hilarious (and with a premonition of play like this for themselves some time?) were helping to keep the spray flying.

The herd master did not have all the 159 other pilot whales as his willing mates, for these whales had an unusual span of fertility: the females were brides at age five but became barren about ten years later, whereas the males were not sexually mature until they were 13 years old but were able to maintain a harem for many years afterward. Both sexes lived approximately 50 years, and so these pilot whales included fertile females but also fairly young grannies, and immatures, both females and males. Like the typical dolphin herds these had their smaller groups—four or five, consisting of four generations of closely related females. In any case all got along well together; their play always seemed to be harmonious.

The pilot whales were so called because they had an irresistible impulse to follow a pilot, a leader—almost any one of their number who dashed away, intent on some goal and keeping ahead of the others. The Whale had a chance to see how suddenly such a migration could start.

He and his friends were still playing around the harem, often watching and apparently finding the high spirits contagious. They weren't the only ones who were aware of the pilot-whale herd, for now a motorboat with three men approached. As they came closer the men stopped the motor, drifted a bit, doubtless to reassure the whales, and then quietly rowed their boat nearer. The pilot whales, alarmed now, used one of the best skills of their species: without a motion, without a sound, they lowered themselves in the water, several feet down— they "let go," as the whalemen said—before they started to swim away. But one of them didn't sink fast enough and the man in the prow raised his gun and shot her.

Immediately she was off—a pilot, a leader! Her quick action, her speed, were enough to send all the rest of the herd tearing after her. The whole ocean seemed full of whales as the entire herd of 160 animals, not small, fled away in the direction the leader was choosing. And that direction, tragically for them, was toward the coast.

The gunner had avoided making his shot a fatal one. For this was a trick men had played on pilot whales for centuries—from the time before there were guns and the hunters must lance the whale they hoped would become a pilot and lead the rest of the herd to destruction. The strategy worked this time too. The men in the boat had known that an injured whale panicked and usually fled to a shore, as distraught whales of many kinds do; and these being pilot whales all the others had followed.

The blue trio swam along after them, not stampeding, only wishing to see what would happen. But they stopped short of the end where the pilot whales, all of them, flung themselves up on the beach—as the men had expected, for waiting there with guns to kill and knives to dismember them were most of the men of the nearest village. They were shouting with triumph, with the exultant prospect of riches, as they carefully caught the oil from the whales' rounded heads which was valued in distant cities as a lubricant for watches.

Luminescence, for tumbling waters were keeping the small plankton creatures excited, surrounded the trio as they returned from the coast to their own wilder ocean. The surface was all alight, as if it burned with a delicate fire. One scientific observer, Charles Darwin, said that the plankton lights in this part of the sea were so bright that the lower part of the sky was rimmed with a pale reflected glow. The blue whales could not see to the distant horizon, but they found on one night that they moved along in a ghost of daylight.

Or wait: on that night were the plankton actually causing the brightness? When the whales repeatedly came up to blow, it seemed that the main source of the light was concentrated; it was in one small part of the sea. As they swam nearer the light became more intense, and excitement, also like fire, ran along the whales' nerves. This was something that few whales had ever seen, and with the curiosity typical of young blues they went close enough finally to learn what was happening.

Two large ships were ablaze. One was a tanker. Trying to reach their destination, Montevideo, too fast, they had collided, a crash instantly followed by an explosion that sprayed oil all over both ships. That oil was now burning.

The ships were encased in fire. It outlined their hulls, their decks, their rigging. Incredible ships, both made of beautiful light!

The whales were reveling in this new and intense experience—flames, seldom seen on an ocean! But oil was now covering the surface, it was spreading farther and farther away from the ships and was getting into the eyes of the blues. Two, the Whale and one of his friends, submerged, but the third was holding himself erect and thus lifting his head and shoulders out of the oil.

Men were jumping down into the water from both the ships, they were swimming along the oil-covered surface—those who could. Others were struggling, giving up, sinking down into the sea, down and down, finally motionless. The Whale and the one who was with him were watching the dying men.

Soon the two blues would have to breathe. Should they come up through the oil again? If they did could they hope that the other would come away with them? He did not have enough of the oil in his eyes to prevent him from seeing the burning ships, and he was still fascinated.

Suddenly, with a *whoosh* like a diabolical wind, all the oil on the sea was afire. The water was covered with brilliant light. It illuminated the depths as the sun never had done and for a few seconds the fish and squids, turtles, porpoises and the larger whales milled about, seeing each other as never before, terrified by the unnatural light above them, revealing too much, throwing them into a panic. Very soon, then, those that could stand the pressure of deeper water dived farther down. For this light on the water was not fascinating—it was more like the end of the world. They felt that they must escape from it, into the sea's more natural twilight.

But the two slowed their precipitous flight. Where was their friend? Why did he not follow them? The others turned back below the blazing surface. And in the brilliant, abnormal light they found him—but he seemed not to be aware of them and did not respond to their calls.

He was acting most strangely and ominously, writhing like a gigantic snake, underwater but clumsily trying to rise into air again. He had been blinded by burning oil, so that when he did return to the top, not seeing, he thrust his head into fire and was convulsed in a spasm of new, searing pain. And then suddenly he was very still, his contorted body relaxing into his usual shape. But he was obviously dead, no longer expressing his agony. He was allowing himself to sink, had drowned actually, the fire having burned the lips of his blowholes so that water poured into his lungs.

The others recognized that they could not help, they could not hold him up into air, and they turned away to the urgent problem of saving themselves. They badly needed to breathe by then but were wary enough of the eerie, sinister light above to feel they must escape from it. Their progress was a demonstration of the Whale's leadership. For his friend probably would have risked trying to blow through the burning surface. But the Whale's strength of purpose, his determination to leave at once and fast was itself an influence. The other, confused and near panic, dreaded losing his guide more than anything else, and so he stayed with the Whale and their relief was, after all, not very far away. The oil had not spread an immense distance from the ships and its farther edges were thinning out. Tossed by waves, they were breaking up into small tufts and splashes of flame. At the very last of the whales' ability to go on without oxygen, they came up among the bright, deadly flowers and gasped in enough air to reach the darkness beyond. There they lay for a long moment, panting, while on the horizon the ships made of light were starting to flicker out.

The episodes of the Whale's first year off the South American coast were typical of the three more years he would spend there—three years before the gracefully waving flukes of a female, appearing and disappearing in waters ahead, would lead him on to a different sea and the prospect of the entirely new life of a mated blue. That development would be more eventful for him than for most other kinds of whales because of the expectation that he and his whale lass would be mating permanently. More emotional growth would be required of him than of the others, more tenderness, more helpfulness, more constancy if he were to succeed in that greatest adventure. For most sorts of whales sex was no more than a casual brief experience. For a blue whale it was a lifetime commitment.

The first necessity was to survive. When a new feeding season approached, he and his friend had to go back into the Southern Ocean where many ships, sailed by clever men, would be searching for whales, especially the largest, to kill them. Increasing, and finally irresistible, hunger would drive these two back to the terrible dangers. In prospect it seemed a choice of deaths, death by starvation or death by harpoon, and for a time starvation seemed preferable. Like most young blues of their age they put off going into the slaughter until hunger, the older and deeper threat, drove them south. They were the last of the migrating blues in that season.

They started out on a course to South Georgia, since that was the only feeding ground either knew. But on the way, between Patagonia and the Falkland Islands, they came upon humpbacks who were feeding without too much interference from men. The two stopped to investigate.

What the humpbacks were eating, straining out of the water with their baleen, were not the familiar little transparent euphausids but different small creatures called lobster-krill by the whalemen. They were an immature stage of the rock lobster *(Munida gregaria)*, smaller than the euphausids, only an inch long, bright red if the whales could have seen colors, and like euphausids with the agreeable habit of congregating in rafts at the surface. The two blue whales, watching the humpbacks, were encouraged to take a few mouthfuls. They didn't like the new food particularly but they didn't dislike it. It didn't taste like the proper nourishment for a blue, and perhaps if they hadn't been young and pliable they would not have continued to eat it, but it did taste like nourishment and best of all the tiny lobsters were here in sufficient quantities so that a mouthful of water filled the whales' baleen with small wriggling creatures waiting there to be sucked off and swallowed. But it would take many millions to supply the two whales for six months. Each of them now weighed about 80,000 pounds.

The blue whales stayed for several weeks near the Falkland Islands. There were whale-catching boats here but not so many that a blue felt himself harassed everywhere that he went. The two gained weight on the lobster-krill though they had to work very hard for that food. It was nowhere concentrated in such quantities as the South Georgia euphausids, and as a few heavy storms from the west suggested the summer's ending, the pair of blues did go on to South Georgia for a last heavy feeding of more familiar krill.

There was something new at the island that year: helicopters. Whales were now being hunted with the huge man-made birds, which would quarter back and forth over the feeding grounds and when they saw a large whale, especially a blue, would stay hovering over it, following everywhere that it went. Already they would have radioed for a catcher boat and soon one would come, tracking its way by the helicopter's position. By the time the two young ones arrived almost every blue that had come to the island that year had been slaughtered. For under the merciless eyes of the helicopters there was no way that a whale could escape.

During the sparse and strenuous feeding on lobster-krill neither of the two youths had gained as much as he should, but they had grown longer. Both were nearly up to the 70 feet of length legal for killing. The Whale was two feet short of it, his friend nearly a foot. That was not a discrepancy easy to estimate from the air, even if helicopter pilots had been eager to observe rules. The two whales arrived in foggy weather and they had two days and nights to gorge themselves on the kind of krill that was right for blues. Then the next day dawned bright and clear.

By eight o'clock one of the helicopters had found them. Everywhere that they swam it flew. Most of the catcher boats were clustered nearer the island and none appeared at once. And the whales, not able to detect radio signals, had no way of knowing that one had been summoned.

The noise of the helicopter was like an assault. When they rose to blow, the mechanical clatter, directly over them and only a few feet above, caused a pain in their ears that was not only physical torment but was disorienting the whales' delicate sense of balance. If it had not been late in the season, when most other whales had been killed or had left, the pilot might not have been quite so determined to get this pair. He might have flown higher, and the difference in decibels might have made it endurable for the blues to stay for another and fatal day. As it was they could not stand the pain and with the Whale leading, the pair of them set about trying to lose the helicopter.

Drawing on memories of his mother's maneuvers, the Whale swam an erratic course. He back-tracked, sped off to one side then the other, circled, swerved up and down, dived and surfaced to breathe for the least possible time. During this dizzy exercise his friend stayed as close to the Whale as he could, though doubtless bewildered, since his own parents were killed before they could teach him the ways to avoid whalemen's boats. Anyway, this enormous overhead bird wasn't a boat. It didn't seem to be shooting harpoons. But its racket clearly suggested menace, enough to have set in motion the Whale's escape tactics.

But not very successfully; everywhere that they went, the helicopter was following. It was almost as if the whales were trailing harpoon ropes, as from a gun on a catcher boat.

And here did come a boat, yes, a catcher boat which also, mysteriously, soon proved impossible to lose. Like the helicopter pilot, its captain followed their every devious move. Catcher boats never had been so infallible before. They sometimes could be outwitted. Why not this one?

Food was forgotten. This was an effort to stay alive, which had begun to seem hopeless. At one desperate time the whales became separated. Then the helicopter and catcher boat chose to follow the one less experienced in dodging. The Whale himself could have gone then, but with his mind set on leaving the krill in these waters now, he must take his friend with him. His friend probably could not find him but the Whale knew where he certainly was: under that helicopter and near the boat. And so the Whale returned to the clatter above and the boat's clanging. He went back into the din he had briefly lost.

A harpoon sliced into the water beside him. It jolted him as, nearby, its murderous head exploded. The Whale was momentarily stunned but, as instantly, instinctively, he went into a depth dive, he left the clamor above far enough to be able to hear that his friend was calling. He answered, they came together again, and then the Whale, abandoning all thought of more feeding here, led the way straight out from the island Shelf, swimming low so that the pilot caught no more than a glimpse of the whales' direction. The two drew on all their capacity to stay under the surface until, by the time they had no choice but to come up for air, they were no longer a target to chase. For the men understood by then that they had driven these whales away.

They swam quickly back to the Falklands and the diminished supply of lobster-krill that at least would await them there.

On the factory ship that had sent out the catcher boat men were dismembering their last blue whale of the season, caught the previous day. It was an old male who had been experienced and wary, who had seen much killing and had assumed that he was able to dodge the catcher boats and always escape them; but the helicopter had defeated him.

As the men were taking his body apart did any one of them wonder what the whale had thought of them? Did it occur to them that he might have had the intelligence to judge men who slaughtered whales and in his own mind condemn them? Or would a blue whale, with no cruel impulse himself, be only mystified?

The men probably did not follow their thought to that uneasy limit. It would be absurd to associate such ideas with the 12 pounds of intricately folded gray tissue that they had cut from the skull of the carcass and that now lay in the slime on the factory ship's floor.

Actually there were men who didn't believe that intelligent animals should have to die so that their bodies might supplement oils from sources like sunflower seeds. Already seven times as much high-grade oil was derived from the seeds as from whales: why not all of it? A fair number of men were critical of the slaughter and many of them were eager to know much more about whales.

What was the cause of the baleen whales growing to be so immense? How had their feeding apparatus evolved? What other adaptations allowed them to fast for six months while still active? To what age did they live? And other questions.

Most fascinating: how intelligent were they? Would it ever be possible for a human being to communicate with a whale, especially one of the huge ones? Could one ever learn from the whales themselves what it was like to be one of the largest creatures ever to live on earth? Since the whales were absolutely unique, it should be a responsibility of human beings—so these men thought—to do everything possible to make sure that their species continued. Some of the men who felt this concern were anxious to observe the large whales themselves, and in that attempt a group had come to stay for a time on the coast of Patagonia.

These were waters where the Argentine government had established a refuge for whales. A few of the southern right whales *(Eubalaena australis)* had discovered that they were safe here and then others, seeing their confident ways, had come and had also stayed, forming a right-whale colony. The two blues, heading north for another season of leisure and growth, were drawn toward this company by seeing a right-whale female who was feeding in the clear blue waves of this unpolluted sea.

She aroused their curiosity because she was a creature the Whale had not seen before, and she was astonishing. She was slightly shorter than he but she had an enormous head—a fourth of her body length—and a gigantic mouth. When she opened it the dark interior was framed with baleen ten feet long and was floored by a tongue so large that it weighed, in fact, 3,000 pounds. She didn't have grooves beneath her chin and so she could not gulp in great mouthfuls of water, as the Whale himself could when his grooves spread apart. Instead she was swimming along near the surface with her mouth constantly open, sieving in plankton as she went forward.

While he watched her the Whale could hear and see others, great shadows moving about through the background water. Then amazingly the Whale saw that a new sort of small animal clung to the flipper of one of the whales and was riding along with it. What could that possibly be? Startled, he had an impression that it might be a man, and he went into a dive and swam farther away from the coast.

But *was* it a man? If not, he would want to know more about it. Gradually he edged back and since none of the others paid any attention to him, he felt safe.

There were three of the strange little creatures. If they were men they were not dressed in the bulky garments of men on the boats. Whatever they wore was black and skin tight. But there was a strange apparatus around the upper parts of their bodies, hoods with masks covering all their faces except the eyes, and tanks on their backs. Their motions in swimming among the whales had none of the clumsiness and abruptness of killer-men's movements. They swam as smoothly and gracefully as fishes and whales, one reason of course being that they were under water, virtually weightless and with the water preventing any quick sort of jabbing or striking. But anyway there was no sign of aggressiveness in these animals, no such sign at all.

And then the small ones discovered the Whale and his friend, and there was a new quickness, almost excitement in their motions as they swam toward the blues. They didn't seem even slightly afraid although the whales were more than ten times their length and 500 times their weight, and how simply they could have been rammed! Neither blue, however, had the least impulse to harm them. They wouldn't anyway, but again the Whale felt about these unknown animals the same indefinable circle of safety surrounding them that he had sensed even about the men at the island. Apparently they were sheltered by it although it was nothing a whale could see or touch. It seemed to belong with the human quality and as this impression came to the Whale, his memory stirred with a faint image of the Negro on the

149

African coast: black, as these creatures were, and with similar unaggressive movements. Probably, yes, all were men.

As the men drew near, they approached more slowly. Tactfully they touched various parts of the Whale's skin and he was startled but not frightened, partly because he assumed from the confidence of the right whales that he too was safe. One of the scientists was gently stroking his face, and then the man allowed the water to lift him so he could see the Whale's blowholes. The Whale needed a breath and as he rose to the surface, the man sprawled across his head and was showered by the spout, but the man showed no fear and he did not leave.

One of the other men drifted up close to an eye of the Whale and looked into it, and for a moment the Whale had an intimation that they were meeting in some mysterious way. These were, in fact, men who were especially interested in animals who were not at all like men but yet were intelligent. Intelligence crossing the species barrier to greet another intelligence was a possibility that intrigued them: two minds making contact, however different the animal forms the intelligence was inhabiting. Minds provided the true brotherhood of the earth's creatures, these men felt. Basic mental material might be the same in all animal lives, only developed further in some than in others and only seeming to have great variety because each mind had to cope with such individual problems—the mind of an elephant, a whale, and a man, for example, fundamentally alike but having to function in such different circumstances. Because octopuses were known to show remarkably intelligent responses, one of the men was making a special study of them, and he was

swimming around enfolded, as it were, in an octopus's embrace—in what seemed the friendliest sort of contact.

The men, who hoped to convince the Blue Whale of their good intentions, would have offered him his favorite kind of food if they could. That being impossible they seemed to be trying to persuade him to remain here. But they were thwarted by the Whale's past experience with killer men. Besides, the Whale could not feel at ease with creatures so unlike himself. Perhaps the gap between species could only be bridged by a human degree of intelligence, although the Blue Whale might have come to feel a sense of fraternity with a few men if he had had many months of association with them—but not in so brief a time as this was going to be.

As the Whale had looked into the eyes behind the glass his curiosity had stirred; but he had no means of satisfying it, no language, no words or ideas that would give him a chance to investigate the thoughts that might be perceived in another's eyes. As the looking continued, he suddenly felt offended, intruded upon, and with one swish of his tail that sent him 30 feet forward, he swam away.

But one of the men was clinging to the small fin on the back of the Whale. He was having a swift and perhaps enjoyable ride but was going too far. He let go and began to swim back to the right whales and the other men. The Whale swung about and finding him with his echo clicks, rose under him and returned him to his fellows. They all showed such pleasure at this evidence of the Whale's understanding and friendliness that he lingered among them for a little while longer.

No other animal ever had seemed so eager to learn

about whales, no other had met his gaze so intently, no other had ever come near and *stayed*. Most of his neighbors in the natural world knew one another only in passing. The men were interested in watching him and he was interested in watching them—a shared wondering about each other that was a quite new experience. In fact the blues' youthful curiosity would be outgrown in a year or two as their maturing blue-whale activities would absorb all their attention. Whalemen, who estimated a blue whale's age by his length, had often commented that the blues up to about 70 feet long were very inquisitive but those of a larger size—literally of a greater age—lost that investigating spirit.

It still was keen enough in the Whale for him to have welcomed this chance to see men who were not killers. Would it be enjoyable if whales and these harmless men could live permanently here in the same part of the sea? Possibly. And yet. . . . It was somewhat uncomfortable to have an association as close as this with a human being, and soon it became disturbing. The two blues would leave now. Giving the men a final but careful splash with his tail flukes, the Whale led the way farther out into the ocean, seeking, hoping to find, waters where only the wild ones were.

9

The Choice

When a creature fasts almost comfortably for six months, it is easy to forget that one day food will again be essential. The whale probably would not look ahead to the future so distinctly, but there would be—there was —first a restlessness, then a sense of emptiness as the energy needed for living, stored in his blubber, was being used up. If he looked as his friend did, he was noticeably thinner by the end of the no-eating months, besides having grown longer. He was a very slim Whale now and more agile, for it was easier to turn and bend with a coat of blubber that was less thick. His motions had become even more serpentine, but he didn't feel right as the third summer approached, and intuition told him that the two of them should go south into waters where there was blue-whale food.

They went first to the sea north of the Falkland Islands where, as before, they found humpbacks contentedly eating lobster-krill. Since it was not the food on which blue whales had grown to be the largest animals ever, lobster-krill did not satisfy the taste preference that blues inherited from millions of ancestors. The two in the western Atlantic had an instinctive urge to return to South Georgia, but instincts can be modified by experience, especially in the more intelligent species, and the killings the two had seen at that island, the threats to themselves and then the excruciating noise of the helicopter the previous year delayed them. They probably would have gone eventually, however, if just at that time a blue-whale female of great age and shrewdness had not come by. Having a motherly temperament, perhaps she was drawn to the two confused adolescents. She stayed around for two or three days and established a little relationship with them. When she started farther along, then, they went with her.

She was not bound for the island the two had known on their first summer and briefly on the second. Her own pastures were farther south—almost directly south of Cape Horn, near the antarctic continent, among other islands that men called the South Shetlands. When the two young whales had been guided to them they found their own favorite euphausids, the only problems being that the quantities were small and the water was glacially cold. Other blue whales were there, a chance for companionship with their own kind and that pleased the two youths. But no one was taking time for much play. All were wildly hungry because this was the accustomed feeding grounds of most of these blues and there was never enough krill to keep them fed adequately. They were thinner than normal blue whales, but actually their slimness helped to protect them from men's predation. One or two factory ships with their catcher boats went south of the Horn, but the islands had many coves and bays and in these and among the many icebergs a smart whale had a good chance to avoid being caught. No doubt there would have been more human hunters here if the migrant blues had been in better condition. All were undernourished so that they would not yield impressive amounts of oil, and most of the whalemen believed that they fared better by staying around South Georgia and killing the lesser whales. At South Georgia there were very few blues but still plenty of fin whales and seis, and until hunting had depleted them to the point where it was not profitable to pursue them, South Georgia was the choice of most whalemen rather than ice fields where the returns were less.

The extremely cold water was rather a hardship to the two young ones. The Whale and his mother had come through ice on their way to South Georgia when he was still nursing, but then being plump and well insulated with blubber, he had not minded the chill. Hunting for krill energetically helped to keep the three-year-olds warm however, and as their blubber thickened, their spirits were high. Toward the end of the season they even took time for a few frolics with other young blues, both males and females. Though the Whale and his friend would not reach an effective interest in the opposite sex for another year, there was a general mood of fun here and they joined in as far as their immaturity allowed. By the time they left to go north again their hunger was far from satisfied, but no harpoon had been fired at them and they did, now, know about a supply of krill that might keep them from ever starving.

For the following months of fasting and further growth they stayed away from the South American coast. They could not escape the clang clang clang of men's ships, heard through all of this ocean, but there were purely wild satisfactions. The pair found a loose population of blues, couples and single whales and even a few young like themselves, scattered over a wide area but in touch by means of their voices.

And the prevalent blue-whale sounds inspired the two to experiment with their own calls. The Whale was amazed by the volume his voice could produce when he tried. It was not as low and resonant as the mountain male's, but it had the same cadence, and as the season progressed his voice began to express the same meaning: *A blue whale here, a male solitary and lonely.*

To creatures who lived in the depths and had depended upon their ears to know what was around them, voices had an importance that a human being could hardly imagine. The Whale's ears, always tuned for listening, were not only picking up his location echoes but sounds of the water itself, its movement, the grind of pebbles and splash of waves and the fall-back of other whales' spoutings: all these were the scenic background against which the living voices stood out, and of these the mightiest were those of the Whale's own species. This was the first time he had been in a gathering of blues who were at ease because they were not being hunted and could enjoy a mild sense of sociability. They were not a close group as humpbacks were usually but were spread out over several hundred square miles. Nevertheless they were communicating, as they easily could since the voice of an adult blue had such great power. At close range in the air it would have blasted a human being right off his feet and in the sea must have blasted some of the smallest organisms right out of existence. Waves of deep sounds like a blue's went through water like ripples, so that some fishes which were composed largely of water and received all through their flesh any strong vibrations around them, must have felt corrugated by the liquid pulses a calling blue whale set in motion. To the Whale himself, the voices gave a new sense of promise. He would be able to do that as well as the best of them, at least after some practice, and so he began sending out messages to whatever blue might be there in the seas rolling around him.

He was only now approaching his sexual maturity, only now sensing that he was hoping to find one blue whale who would be more interesting than others. And it may have been that message, instinctively directed to a blue female, that told the Whale himself that he wanted something or someone. His voice, whose tone was saying, *Where can I find you? Or will you come to me?* could have put a definite meaning into the new kind of hunger that was making him feel dissatisfied. Calling to someone unknown may have been the inspiration for more swimming about, now—no longer just enjoying himself in an idle way but seeking—for what he would know when he found it, or her.

His blue companion was also using his voice but less urgently. He stayed with the Whale in his search but with his own sexual impulse developing rather more slowly. The Whale continued to call and his voice had the special quality due to his age: *A YOUNG whale here . . . lonely.*

He was answered remarkably soon. The newcomer did not call—she just appeared one morning, her presence first known by her echo clicks focusing over his body, as he could feel. They were like fingers by which a human being, silent in darkness, might grope to find another, and when the clicks touched the Whale's skin he stopped moving in order that she could more easily come to him. As soon as her faster clicks told him that she was nearer he spoke, a talking rather than calling voice, and almost at once she was there, passing back and forth near him as each tested the sense of the other's presence.

The Whale followed her while she was swimming around and before long he managed a glide so that his skin slid over hers. The touch was at the same time pleasing and disappointing. He tried the same test again, more slowly so that their bodies were in contact a little longer. Again the effect was both right and not right and simultaneously the two whales turned and swam away from each other. For what was missing, although both were ready for sex, was compatability.

Human beings are often surprised to learn that courting wild animals can be very discriminating. Domestic animals, whose true temperaments have been distorted through long centuries of man-manipulated breeding, are usually deprived of emotional expression until any coupling whatever is welcomed. But in nature it is not true that just any male and female accept each other. Many are so selective that they refuse available sex until a partner wholly sympathetic is found. Surprisingly often none *is* found, so that more than a few wild creatures remain unmated—40 percent is the estimate among passerine birds. And so it was not strange that the Whale drew back from his first association with a possible female. With his sensitive intuition he would not make a mistake and form a pair bond that would not be permanently satisfying to both of them.

During that fourth fasting season he found two other females of the right age for mating. Neither was promising as a lifelong companion. A total of only three was not an encouraging number, because the subtropical waters here had once been the playground of thousands of blue whales and many new families had been established each year. The Whale's inherited instincts prepared him for the expectation that he would have similar luck. That he didn't may have been one of the reasons why he led his bachelor friend away to the south earlier than they would have gone otherwise.

They eased the worst pangs of hunger by stopping around the Falklands briefly for lobster-krill and then went on past the Horn. Knowing the way this year they spent less time in searching and found some moderately dense rafts of euphausids fairly soon. They were close to the antarctic continent, from which icebergs were breaking away almost continually. In the antarctic gales these bergs, miles in breadth at first, soon broke up into fleets of majestic white ghost ships, moving in stately grandeur northeast to warmer seas and their doom as meltwater. Here they still held aloft their proud spars of ice, and on days when the sun caught on the icebergs' rigging the air was brilliant with sparkling light.

The euphausids were scattered among the icebergs and had to be hunted energetically, but at least the ice made a labyrinth of hiding places from catcher boats along the white shorelines. And there the water remained fairly still, even so quiet that the small shrimps could form rafts, fortunately for whales since a whole raft could be gulped in at once. A few other blues were here, not many but a dozen or so . . . and what, then, was unique about one whose flukes waved ahead of him as the Whale was swimming along a canal between the halves of a berg that had split apart? She was evidently intending to come out at the other end of the passageway, as he was himself, but though the pulse of her tail was regular, its two flukes had a somewhat uneven tilt, more than the usual torque, and to compensate and keep herself on a straight course this whale had a most fascinating swing to the end of her body. It was certainly the most subtle swimming the Whale had seen, and with an extra thrust of his own tail he drew up beside her.

Startled, she dived to swim in deeper water. Ahead the two halves of the iceberg were closing together and so she had to come back to the top, but the canal at the surface was closing too and the stranger seemed flustered, perhaps frightened momentarily. The Whale touched her reassuringly and then took five or six quick breaths as a hint of the way they should try to escape. The female followed his lead and, as he dived, she was close behind him.

It was necessary to go half a mile down in order to get under the submerged mass of the berg. Both of them were experienced enough in depth diving to know what to do: come up very slowly. They could not start to rise however until they were out from under the ice and there were some tense moments while the whales were needing desperately to breathe. The Whale himself set the pace. He swam at the female's side, his body close to hers for encouragement, even touching hers toward the end of their rise when she was making small frantic movements in her great need for oxygen. After the long dive was over they lay at the surface, panting, while their bodies readjusted to a restored supply of air and relief from the water's heavy pressure below. Indeed they lay there rather longer than necessary, the female relaxing, it seemed, in the Whale's protectiveness and he sensing his wonder at the appeal of this new young creature. He gently put one of his flippers across her shoulder and she did not dart away.

They were lying in fact in a rather dense patch of krill and before long the female started to feed. The delicious moments were past and the three whales spent the rest of the day taking in nourishment.

During the short polar night, which was only a dusk, not darkness, the three whales rested, dozing, merely rousing enough to tilt up their tails when their blowholes lowered beneath the surface. Because they were all thin, they did not float quite as successfully as if they had had the typical blues' coats of blubber. But the female and the other bachelor lightly slept for more time than the Whale himself did. He was always listening for the beat of a catcher-boat's engines, for if one came closer the three

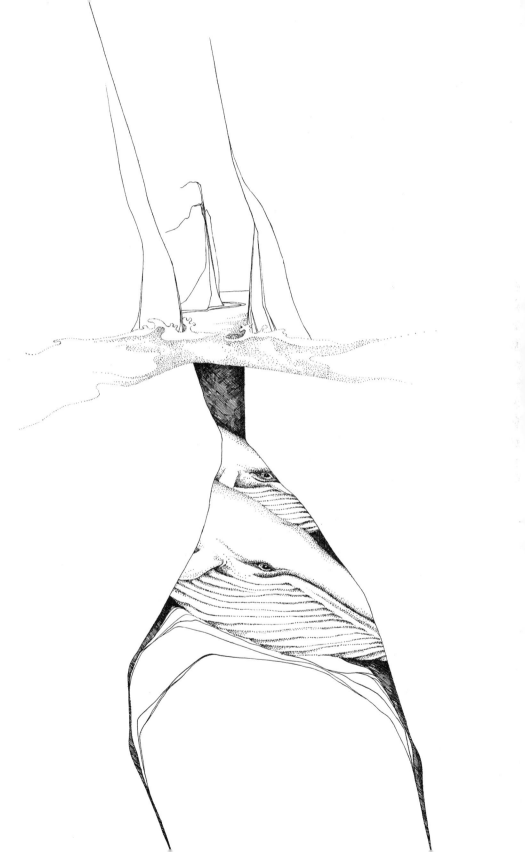

must seek safer water. To guard his own life was not his only concern now. He had come, suddenly and surprisingly, to feel that the safety of this female was as important, at least, as his own.

That became the pattern of the following days: finding and eating krill among the byways of the icebergs, dodging away from catcher boats when necessary, which was not all the time, resting during the hours when no boats were near and meanwhile becoming used to the feeling that the three of them somehow belonged together. The whale lass did not try to get away from the two males, for neither was courting her so persistently as to interfere with the need in these months to put on as much weight as possible. She was the hungriest of the three, nature no doubt tending to prompt her. For she was of mating age, and if she took the next normal step she would need enough blubber to nourish herself and a young one growing within her. It was not practical for a young female to be as slender as she was, even though she could move with a more attractive grace by not having a somewhat stiff coat of blubber nearly a foot thick all over her body. She didn't have that—much less, in fact, for she never had found such a feast as the one at South Georgia. But her increased hunger, now that she was older and longer, kept her eating obsessively. With luck she would have a large enough store of food in her body for whatever demands the next year might bring.

The Whale, without this particular need, kept eating but less compulsively. His other hunger was becoming more urgent, though more gradually than with species that mated abruptly and without emotional preparation. Among animals that were monogamous the custom of

164

longer courtships was the rule, for nature would not risk lifelong attachments between pairs who had made quick and chancy attachments. Since a pair of wolves, or gibbons, or blue whales, among other creatures, were to be monogamous, their congeniality not only had to be tested well but, besides, they needed to grow into the deeper devotion that such a pair bond would require.

During their summer among the icebergs the Whale seemed more sure of this female's suitability than she did of his. Of the kind of interest that would be expressed by her motions there was not a great deal as yet—less than of his. But she was willing to have him be near her and occasionally to express his desire by running a flipper down her side or lightly touching her with his mouth. If he seemed too insistent she dived and came up some distance away. But then when he came again to her side she did not seem to be clutching any resentment. She even showed small signs of affection at times, though annoyingly she was friendly to the other bachelor too. His sexual maturity had progressed remarkably fast since they had found this enchanting creature. With less initiative in all ways than the Whale, he had not seemed a serious rival in the beginning, but he had become very attentive to the female in his mute patient way, and she showed some appreciation by feeding or resting near him. Then the Whale often would push between them, acting as if he had priority, although he didn't, not at this stage.

Thus, with its great promise and now and then with anxiety, the feeding season moved on to its end. The nights had become very cold indeed, and the wintry months had their warning in the frost flowers that were

beginning to form in the water. Lovely small crystal pom-
pons were clustering wherever the waves were not bois-
terous, and as the whales ate voraciously they began
taking as many morsels of ice as of krill into their mouths.
There was only one thing to do—leave. The bachelors
would go wherever the lass went. And where would that
be?

She proceeded straight up into and through the
tumultuous waters that bordered Cape Horn. Obviously
she was not going to lead the males past the Falkland
Islands, where they would have paused for a further
feeding, but there were some of the lobster-krill among
the scattering of islands at the tip of the continent too,
and they all stayed there long enough to fill up some
further chinks in their hunger. None of them felt completely satisfied. The males' blubber was an inch or two
thinner than it had been last year at this time, and the
female lacked the proper weight for a blue of her age.
Every year, as they grew in size, it seemed that they
slipped a little farther behind what would have been
sufficient nourishment for their fasting months. But that
was a worry that could be postponed to the time, five or
six months from now, when the ice of the polar winter
would seem too slow in uncovering the new feast of krill.
For the present there was this lovely girl-whale and the
two males both desiring her.

Much that was here would have interested the
Whale in the years when he was not absorbed in a per-
sonal quest. Trees, a small forest on one of the shores; for
a short way they swam along with beech trees extending
their branches almost directly over them. What would he
have made of that at the time when he was curious about

every new thing? Sea lions were in the water, the males heaving their clumsy bulk through the waves, chasing the rock-hopper penguins that jumped down off the rocky shores and then kept springing out of the water as if they were trying to soar like the flying fish. Their aspiration only landed them in the jaws of the sea lions who, almost uniquely among animals, seemed to kill for sport, since they did not eat most of their victims though vultures were there and did. The three great whales hardly gave the sea lions a glance but they shied away from two boats, pitching and wallowing in the gale-driven waves as they rounded the Horn. To a blue whale all boats were crewed by agents of death, though these two were only trying to win a round-the-world race.

And then the bachelors learned where their delight-ful guide was taking them: into the unexplored waters of the Pacific Ocean, northward along the coast of Chile. The males were not reluctant to be adventuring into a different scene. The ocean everywhere was home to them in the sense of being their element, but the currents and depths and inhabitants here were unlike those of seas they had known before. And they had a bright impulse to wander, perhaps an extension of their juvenile ques-tioning. Besides, there was that irresistible flutter of un-dulating flukes in the waves ahead of them.

When the wind-driven current of the Pacific Ocean reached the west coast of South America, it had had a 5000-mile sweep unbroken by any islands, the widest stretch of clear sea anywhere in the world. As that racing current hit the land mass, then, it swirled upward with a force that dug an offshore ditch, the Chile–Peru Trench, more than five miles deep. And it brought to the surface many strange dwellers of the remote seabed, and also a wealth of mineral food stuffs so nourishing that fishes thrived as in no other place on earth. The fish supported millions of diving birds, so many that their droppings, guano in heaps up to 30 feet thick, fertilized farm crops in every country. Peru, Chile's neighbor, harvested the small fish called anchovetas directly and turned them into cattle feed that went a fair way toward nourishing the world's livestock. Many millions of human beings were fed by the bounty of those currents off South America.

There were whales in those waters too, also thriving on the minerals as transformed into plankton. As the three from the Antarctic sped northward they passed gatherings of sperm whales, all fat and well-nourished because of the numerous fish, and many humpbacks. But no feast was available to the blues because krill was not there. It still was true that euphausids were their essential diet and they had passed beyond the Convergence where euphausids turned down from the surface to the deeper, warmer current that would take them back to their winter habitat near the antarctic continent. From there, making a circular tour, they would go northward again in the spring. If the three blue whales could adjust to being thinner, to being a little hungry most of the time, next year perhaps they could return to the sea of beautiful ice and again in comparative safety find lagging krill that had not migrated up to South Georgia. Theirs was an austere life but at this time a supremely happy one for these three who were finding their satisfaction in the company of each other.

When the whale lass felt ready to have a courtship proceed she told the males in her language of motion. In that she was like most mammals except that being a blue whale, she already had the vocabulary of grace. There only needed to be a little more fluency in her swimming, a sharper curve when she turned down for a dive, a more wayward bending now to one side, now to the other as she circled or spiraled; a somewhat friskier splashing, a swifter dash away when inviting pursuit. What words of even the most articulate tongue could say it more eloquently: *Catch me!*

The Whale was enchanted and his own motions had become eloquent: *Just let me!* He had the sense, typical of a born leader, that the prizes in life were his natural right —not a right automatically but because it would be his way to win them.

The only troubling element was the fact that the other bachelor was also enthralled. He might not have much initiative in exploring seas but in exploring ways to be ingratiating he was not backward. When the Whale swam beside the female with a forceful thrust that meant, *Stay with me,* she was apt to drop behind and even turn to his rival. The Whale was the more compelling but the other was very gentle.

The ocean here seemed a suitable scene for some great consummation, for everything was of excessive proportions. The waves were so huge that during a storm the breaking surf could be heard 20 miles inland. The mountains along the shore were so high (to 23,000 feet) that night lay long over the shoreward sea before the sun finally came over those heights. The upwelling of mineral nutriments from the Trench were so rich that not only did they ultimately support the most numerous colonies of sea birds on earth; but fishes like tunas grew to 1500 pounds weight.

Near an island, Más-a-Tierra, the three whales saw an amazing episode. The island is known to men because an English sailor, Alexander Selkirk, who was stranded there, was supposed to have inspired Daniel Defoe's *Robinson Crusoe*. What was observed by the whales however, had a more dramatic ending. A fish attacked a boat, causing two men to drown, an incident that even briefly distracted the whales' attention from their romantic concerns.

The men, Indians, were in a small boat and had come out to spear swordfish. The swordfish were not as numerous here as they would be off the coast of Peru, but one was circling around the boat and the men kept hurling their bamboo harpoons, their *chuzos,* though not with enough success to kill or even seriously injure the swordfish. The men, so small, were very daring. A whale would have expected them to show more caution, for the swordfish, in this realm of giants, had a stout body ten feet long and his sword extended another ten feet. It was like a dual fought with spears, both of similar length: astonishing that the men seemed so confident.

Quite suddenly the fighting swordfish was joined by another that darted in and before the men could attack it drove its sword through the bottom of the boat. The sword might have broken off but the fish withdrew it, leaving a hole, and now there was a most frantic change in the Indians' actions. One tore off his shirt and tried to stuff it into the hole, while the other man started to paddle away toward the distant shore. But the swordfish both followed and kept attacking the boat.

Now the Indians did show fear, for the boat had begun to sink. For a time the men worked at attempting to plug the holes, and with both absorbed in trying to keep out the water, neither could paddle. The waves were steep and soon they were breaking over the boat. When the boat was entirely under the surface the men gave up. One seemed to be kneeling and the water soon covered him; the other stood upright with his hands clasped above his head and his eyes turned to the sky. When he too disappeared the whales left to continue along up the coast. But those swordfish: they had been a sight to stay in the mind of the Whale. He had seen swordfish in the Pernumbuco Basin, but small ones. Could a Whale ram a fish with such a formidable weapon as those of the fish in this ocean?

Where was the whale lass leading them? She went ahead, on a course that had all the appearance of being remembered. And then off the coast of Peru she proceeded no farther. Instead she swung around in a leisurely way as if glad to be back in what probably were her home waters.

She seemed at ease among the strange creatures here, none for a blue whale to fear of course but such monsters of their own kind that they were a bit disconcerting. Besides the 1500-pound tunas and 20-foot swordfish, there were octopuses so large that when they spread themselves out they were like curtains hung in the ocean. The giant squids from the seabed had to be recognized by echo clicks since they only came up for their surface feeding at night. Although they were formed like the small squids seen everywhere, these were 50 feet long with ten arms each as thick as the thigh of a man. Giants of many kinds, in a world of mammoth proportions but the largest were still the blues, all three now approaching lengths of 80 feet plus the 10 feet of their flukes and with more growth ahead of them. Young blue-whale parents were often still growing themselves while they were supervising a first-born infant.

The Whale was finding it very hard to wait until the female was ready for the commitment that, to him, seemed without question right and inevitable. Why did there have to be this delay? All her motions told him that she was ready, although she still was not willing to let him lie with his body against her body, stroking it, skin to skin, in the many ways that were possible to a supple blue whale.

The other bachelor did not try to persuade her into these further delights. He was just always there, near her with tireless devotion, awaiting her wish. But the Whale himself kept trying to show her what she was missing. During their nighttime rest, when they all dozed at the surface, the Whale often came close and let his body glide along hers. He did not try to clasp her with flippers, he did not encircle her, as his limber body would let him do. He was just demonstrating what the next expression of their devotion could be.

Their devotion? She had only said, with her motions, that she was interested, not that she had accepted him as her mate—for life, as it would be. And then one morning when the Whale came fully awake, she was not there. With an alarmed searching he swam everywhere in the nearby waters. The other male, instantly alert, also was seeking her. Where could she be and why had she gone?

She hadn't gone far. She would not have led the males here, she would have lost them weeks earlier if she had not felt that one of them would make a satisfactory life partner. But which one? She needed to be away from both for a little while, waiting until her intuition would give her the answer.

The more passive male was more comfortable to be with. There was no high-pressuring in his behaviour. He was just always faithfully near and a female responded gratefully to companionship so dependable. Life was difficult for a whale that could only feed where the krill was scarce. Only a few generations ago a blue whale could live with confidence, but no longer. One's natural ease was undercut by uncertainty and to have a partner whose affections so obviously would be reliable tempted her. He did not stir her sexually but her own urges were not intense. For that kind of fulfillment one needed to be well fed—perhaps because a species without reassurance about the future would lack the impulse to give offspring to it. With many animals, past and present, extinction seemed to have come about for that reason.

But that Whale! Though he too had not had adequate food this last season, what vitality could be felt in all that he did! When he was swimming along with the other two, how his tail would *swoop* up and down so that he constantly was ahead and had to be idle while they caught up. He kept diving and then rising so close to her that she was constantly being startled, though not unpleasantly. He splashed through the water on the left of her and then—so fast!—on the right. He enclosed her in

a network of unexpected dives and surfacings which prevented the other male from sedately swimming along at
her side—and was that his purpose? It seemed like a
game, everything he did seemed like a game: his quick
touchings and speeding away before she could show dis-
pleasure. He dared to pass her so near that his skin slid
all the way down her skin: curiously pleasurable but not
if he did it too often. He was very stimulating and could
she respond adequately? Did she feel equal to so challenging a relationship?

The female was hearing his call many times a day.
She was only a few miles away, too far to be found with
his echo clicks but within range of a normal voice. His
was poignant. It was like an intimate touch. The other
male too would call but not so often or urgently. That
voice only said, *Where are you?* The Whale's said, *Come
to me!*

She went. When the Whale roused one morning
there she was, just as if she never had been away. Electric
with his delight he swam in every direction that could
possibly bring him close to her: up, down, along her
sides, under her belly, over her back, not once touching
her but surrounding her with the swirling currents he
trailed. She held herself still as long as she could, but
quivering, and then, with outbursting emotion she flung
herself into responding to his excited movements.She
could follow his lead in the most subtle interweaving of
bodies; down and up, to one side and the other they spun
and swept, buoyed by the water and propelled by the
grace learned through years of play with only the sea for
a partner.

And then they were circling around on the surface,

gathering strength, moving slowly now . . . slowly, the circles narrowing as the two tensely contained the emotion building within them—until, with the circles reaching their center, the whales united with an explosive surge that raised them right out of the water, face to face out and up in the air, the sunlight, towering into the sky, two of the earth's greatest creatures lifted aloft by their ecstasy.

The tremendous thrust that had shot them clear of the sea, all but their flukes, could not hold them out and separating they fell sidewise back into the waves. The dazzle of spray was like a splintering of the sun itself. And then, with the first of such events over, they relaxed, lying together, recovering breath, flippers embracing and skin touching all the way down the long length of their bodies. It was a pause before a new life began for them, a new life because they were mated blue whales now.

They paid attention to nothing and no one except each other. The bachelor was still there, although he had withdrawn to an impersonal distance. Would he leave the others entirely or perhaps stay in the background, becoming an uncle to any offspring? His temperament might allow that, for he seemed born to a life of undemanding devotion—though no one could know whether too little nourishment had contributed to his passivity.

When the pair stirred again, they moved peacefully, the female swimming ahead, seeking nothing. The Whale followed, just now wanting only the sight of her, of her flukes which were not forcing their way through the water, only fanning with a delicate swing that sent her on but not far or fast.

Changing their tilt she rose to the surface to breathe. The Whale drew alongside her, stroking her with a glide, back to repeat, and again. It roused the female enough so that she turned below in a shallow dive, the Whale beside her, soon taking the lead in a beautiful entwined swirling. They were not only the earth's largest creatures but probably the most harmonious, the most perfectly in tune with each other.

The duet of motion began to gain speed. And faster: now they have begun to circle again near the top, with the curves drawing in to a center and with more splashing, coming even more quickly than the first time to excitement—

Summoned by the noise and infected by the feverish emotion, a swordfish sped up from below. Like a harpoon his spear was plunged into the female's side. If she could have remained motionless the fish might have withdrawn it but her convulsive start broke the sword off and before either whale could ram him the fish was away.

It took a moment for the two whales to adjust to the new situation. As the stunned female lay motionless then, he circled her twice and when she didn't respond he lobtailed and slapped her side. Only then, seeing blood spurt from her wound, did he fully realize what had happened. When a swordfish attacks a whale he seems always to try to place the stab just behind a flipper. That had been done this time and the ten-foot sword was implanted squarely between her lungs and her heart, nicking both.

Quickly! At once she must speed away toward the land. And quickly, *quickly*. The shore was 12 miles away and she must reach it before all her strength was gone.

The Whale swam beside her and on the other side was the bachelor friend who had seen what occurred and apparently sensed that he might be needed.

The shore was in sight but the water still deep when the wounded whale had to stop. Her spouts had become "chimney fires" now from all the bleeding inside her lungs and she was losing still more blood from the slit in her heart. For a few moments she lay at the surface but then, unable to hold herself there, she began to sink. Instantly the two males swung beneath her, lifting her into the air on their shoulders. As all blue whales do, they understood that she had to have oxygen and they would hold her up there as long as was necessary. When one had to breathe, himself, the other continued supporting her. Mutely, in the way of the wild ones in even the most desperate situations, the two fought for the female's life.

There was something new in the water: the sound of a boat's engines churning. For the red spouts of the injured whale had been seen on shore.

She clearly was dying. No more spouts rose in the air, and then without doubt she was dead. The bachelor sensed that she was and the next time the Whale replaced him below her, he dived deeply and swam away. The Whale would not give up. Alternately he tried to keep her head out in the air and stopped to swim around her, from side to side, desperately seeming to plead with her —*Only breathe again, only live!*

The boat was very near now, a catcher boat from a whaling shore station. But still the Whale did not leave. He could have but would not. Self-preservation is called the first and strongest instinct, but it is not among blue whales—not when a loving heart makes the choice.

The men killed him of course. It did not occur to them—it never occurred to any whalemen—to hold their fire because they respected devotion so great that a whale would accept certain death to comfort a mate.

The harpoon, crashing into his head, did its work almost instantly, but not before he had rammed the boat with a blow that made it shudder from end to end, a blow that displaced the harpoon so that it fell away and the men had no time to load another. They lost the female as well, for by then she was too far under the surface. The Whale and his mate sank together into the twilight depths of the welcoming sea.